The Green Thread

ALSO BY KAREN LUECK

Cheering for the Good: Leading When it Matters

The Green Thread

Reclaiming Our Spiritual Authority

KAREN LUECK

goodness
press

Published by goodness press, La Crosse, WI

Edited and designed by Girl Friday Productions
www.girlfridayproductions.com

Cover design: Ashton Smith
Project management: Kim Kent
Editorial production: Alyssa Brillinger
Image credits: © Pexels/Marina Leonova

The Scripture quotations contained herein are from the New
Revised Standard Version Bible, copyright ©1989 by the Division of
Christian Education of the National Council of Churches of Christ
in the USA, and are used by permission. All rights reserved.

ISBN (hardcover): 979-8-9929213-0-4
ISBN (paperback): 979-8-9929213-1-1
ISBN (ebook): 979-8-9929213-2-8

First edition

This command which I am giving you today
is not too wondrous or remote for you.
It is not in the heavens, that you should say,
"Who will go up to the heavens to get it for us and tell us of it,
that we may do it?"
Nor is it across the sea, that you should say,
"Who will cross the sea to get it for us and tell us of it,
that we may do it?"
No, it is something very near to you,
in your mouth and in your heart, to do it.

(Deuteronomy 30:11–14)

CONTENTS

THE CHALLENGE

In 2020, the whole world found itself in a crisis—one whose fallout led many of us to engage in serious personal reflection. For me, a period of self-examination had begun even before the COVID-19 pandemic hit.

Two years earlier, I had completed a four-year term as president of the Franciscan Sisters of Perpetual Adoration in La Crosse, Wisconsin, where I am a member of a community of "women religious," the modern term for Catholic sisters previously known as "nuns." After the end of my term, I had written a book about my experience of leadership, *Cheering for the Good: Leading When It Matters*, and had recently begun to wonder what I was being called to next.

Then the pandemic hit, and I found myself, along with everyone else, living through one of the most devastating and challenging times ever. In the US, we were assaulted not only by the COVID pandemic and the fear, chaos, and rage surrounding it, but also by a new spate of police violence against unarmed Black men and women. Then on May 25, 2020, in Minneapolis, just two and a half hours north of La Crosse, an unarmed Black man named George Floyd was murdered in plain view of a crowd of people, most of whom had cell phones. The resulting videos went viral and lit a powder keg of outrage throughout the city and country. Massive demonstrations followed in cities everywhere.

As a member of the Franciscan community and as an author of a book on leadership, I knew it was important for people to step up. But I wasn't clear what my own next steps should be. I wanted to do something to stop this insanity and show my support for my Black brothers and sisters. But what could I do? I was haunted for months by my inability to act while the world was burning. Gradually, through prayer and contemplation, I finally came to a new understanding of what God was asking of me. Three challenges that I had heard or read resonated in my heart: one from my Black sisters and brothers; the second from the founder of the Franciscan order, Saint Francis of Assisi; and the third from the Dalai Lama. Quite a combination, I must say! Here's how the challenges came to me.

First, around that time, I was driving in my car when I heard a program on Minnesota Public Radio about the aftermath of George Floyd's murder. Many white people, like me, were asking what they could do to show solidarity at this time of persecution and outrage. The Black guests on the show thanked the white individuals for their concern and support, but redirected them, advising them that before they attempted to engage in their own efforts to end racism, they should first heal themselves. This counsel echoed what writer, poet, and activist Audre Lorde already said back in 1984 as quoted in her book, *Sister Outsider*: "I am myself—a Black woman warrior poet doing my work—come to ask you, are you doing yours?" (41)

Second, as a Franciscan, I have often repeated over the years the words Saint Francis of Assisi allegedly uttered to his followers on his deathbed in the thirteenth century: "I have done what was mine to do. Now it is time for you to do what is yours to do." I realized now that this question of what one's work to do is, was the very dilemma with which I was wrestling.

Still, I felt left up in the air about what these two challenges meant. The third challenge, from the Dalai Lama, made it somewhat clearer. Around this time, I happened to reread two books by women authors that had inspired me some years earlier, and I recognized that both authors, Kathe Schaaf and Sharon Blackie, had cited the words the Dalai Lama reportedly spoke at the 2009 Vancouver Peace Summit: "The world will be saved by the Western woman."

This quote was controversial at the time. Online there was some negative reaction to the word "saved," pointing out that we humans are not meant to save anyone. But when I looked into what the Dalai Lama's talk was about, I understood that he was referring to the fact that many Western women have more access to good education, health care, and economic opportunities than other people in the world, and he was urging them to step up and use these privileges to make the world a better place.

I recently found a quote by Marianne Hughes, in 2009 the executive director of the Interaction Institute for Social Change (IISC), which conveys an understanding of the Dalai Lama's talk similar to mine. She states the following:

> I am not entirely sure what he [the Dalai Lama] meant . . . but I am wondering if, when he travels across the globe and sees so many of our sisters impoverished and repressed, he sees Western women in a position to speak out for justice and . . . to take loving care of the planet and its people. (article by Linda Lowen)

Whenever a group of similar quotes like these shows up on my radar in a relatively short period of time, I take this to be a sign to me that I need to stop and pay attention. And I did.

An Invitation to White Women

Living in the United States, I believe the "Western women" quote applies particularly to white Western women. That is because white women are the women who have "white privilege," whether we admit we do or not. White privilege refers to the unearned advantages that white people have in society simply because of their race. We white people may sometimes refuse or neglect to point out injustices that non-whites are enduring, often because we fear losing our privilege. White women especially have learned to stay silent. Too often, we have gone along with unjust systems rather than challenging them. As the Dalai Lama and the others whose voices I quoted have pointed out, we are now being challenged to do our own inner healing, to quit playing it safe, to risk being vulnerable, to claim our voices. Only in that way can we partner with other people working for justice.

None of this will be easy. Huge issues await us if we rise to meet this challenge, including confronting our own deep fear of being ourselves, our own rejection of ourselves as powerful agents, our own intergenerational trauma, and our own complicity in keeping the white male power system in place. This is dangerous work. Are we Western white women up for this? Am I up for this?

As I pondered this powerful call throughout the three years of writing this book, I unknowingly uncovered a deep place within me that I didn't know was there. I could feel palpable fear and deep resistance. *What will I find out about myself on this journey? Do I even want to embark on it? Do I want to let go of my privileged place as a white woman? Can I endure the pushback I may receive by challenging the system?* But throughout this deep questioning, I knew that the Spirit of God was calling me to this exploration and would walk with me the whole way.

Choosing to Heal

I embarked on much research to see how other people had come to discover what was needed to bring about their healing. I learned from historians, psychologists, sociologists, and others that recognizing my own intergenerational trauma and incomplete family history was necessary to begin the healing. But I really had no clue what this meant for me, since I didn't know much of my ancestral history. So, research into my family history became the next step in my work. As you will read, I learned much about the intergenerational trauma that has both infected my life and kept me from moving forward. And I also found a way to heal from it.

I have divided this book into three sections: 1) my research into my ancestors and my familial trauma; 2) the way this trauma affected my ancestors through the centuries and the resilience that they were able to embrace; and 3) how this trauma and resilience still show up today, and what healing looks like.

I have attempted to be vulnerable about the process of my own healing in order to give you, my readers, a sense of how you, too, can heal the intergenerational trauma that may hamper your life and embrace your full personhood, so that together we can bring healing to the planet. The emphases in the book will come from my perspective—that is, as a white, Midwestern, German American, Catholic Christian woman religious. Each of you will have to embrace your own unique background and experience in order to bring about personal healing.

For me, the fear is still there, and I'm sure I'll encounter many surprises along the way. Still, I trust that the Spirit of God will continue to show me the way forward to healing and give me strength to be vulnerable, loving, funny, and compassionate to myself and to all others on the journey. I welcome you to join me.

Part One

1

Early Exploration

The first time I really began to delve into my family history in a systematic way was back in 1988, in a class on family systems theory that I took in the graduate Pastoral Counseling program at Loyola University Chicago. As part of our studies, we were asked to create a genogram, a map of one's family tree that includes individual characteristics, relationships, hereditary patterns, and cultural events that influence who we are.

Using what family history records my parents had at home—including baptismal records, photos with notes on the back, newspaper clippings of funeral announcements—and other information that had been passed down from the time my ancestors emigrated to the US, I was able to trace both sides of my family back to the late eighteenth century in northwest Germany. I learned my ancestors' names, and I learned that they had all been Catholic. All, with a few exceptions, were farmers or farmers' wives, all had large families, and all were rooted firmly in one place for a long time.

I brought this meager information from my Loyola days to the present search for my ancestors, and, in doing so, I realized that my ancestral knowledge was made up of a lot of silence. My parents and grandparents, probably like many families, didn't talk much about their immediate ancestors; they spoke even less about their ancient ancestors. I'm not sure they even knew who they were. My family was not gifted in the way of families from other cultures and religions who pray to their ancestors regularly and see them as an integral part of their daily lives. The result was that I didn't know about their actual lives, their feelings, their challenges, their resilience (or lack thereof), anything that really made them human. I didn't get to know them as people with whom I could have a relationship. But this didn't stop me from wondering about them. I found myself with many questions. *What were the events in their lives, both positive and negative, that shaped who they were? What did they fear? What did they enjoy? How did they deal with life's problems? How am I like them?*

I came to the journey of exploration and healing I described in "The Challenge" with very little information. So I decided to start with myself. I wanted to explore who I was and what I had come to know about myself and my immediate family, and thus hopefully find hints about who my ancestors were.

If you choose to embark on a similar journey, you must begin with your own story. In these pages, I will reveal my story and my process of getting in touch with my ancestors, but every person's story is their own. This point became clear to me after I read Sharon Blackie's book *If Women Rose Rooted: The Journey to Authenticity and Belonging.* In the book, Blackie, writer, mythologist, and psychologist, explores her own Irish roots. She states:

> In our own Western societies, we are seeing
> more calls for a return to native wisdom, but
> we cannot live by the worldviews of other

cultures, which are rooted in lands and histories that have little relationship with our
own. . . . We have our own guiding stories,
and they are deeply rooted in the heart of our
own native landscapes. (19)

Let me share a little bit of my own story and how it impacted my experiences of longing and healing. Perhaps reading this part of my journey will inspire you to explore your
stories and see how they may ground you and open you up to
new possibilities for healing.

My Story

I grew up in the 1950s–'60s on a farm near New Vienna, a
small town in northeastern Iowa. My dad farmed 220 acres
of cropland (corn, oats, hay), raised hogs and some sheep, and
milked dairy cows. My mom was a housewife and mother to
five children while also growing a huge garden, tending chick-
ens, feeding the threshers, and generally helping out on the
farm whenever and wherever needed. My two brothers and
two sisters became my primary playmates as no other children
lived near us.

I am a fourth-generation German American with strong
roots in our community and in the Catholic Church. Like
many German Americans, my siblings and I were discouraged
from sharing feelings and vulnerabilities. It was important for
everything to be neat and tidy, and feelings could get so messy.
My parents both had a strong sense of duty, and they worked
hard. Of the two of them, my father took work more lightly. He
always found time to relax and socialize with friends in town.
My mother, on the other hand, seemed to be constantly working. I don't think I ever saw her sit down to relax and enjoy

herself. We kids used to call her the "martyr." She did everything for her husband and her children. She never seemed to express her own needs.

Mom did make clear, though, that she had a great love of school. After finishing grade school in the 1930s, she desperately wanted to attend high school. But her parents, like other parents at the time, instead sent her out to help her married siblings' families when they had new babies. Mom felt deeply the pain of their decision, even into her later years.

To compensate for what happened in her own family, Mom decided to never let me as her first daughter be enslaved by duty and work. Sure, I had chores like cleaning, drying the dishes, taking care of the younger kids, and mowing the lawn. But Mom went overboard in shielding me. When I offered to help with the housework, she told me to "go out and play." When I wanted to learn to cook, she told me that she worked better in the kitchen on her own. I started to feel worthless. Out of a desire to be a "good girl," I wanted to help my mother and relieve her burdens, but she wouldn't let me. So that left me feeling selfish, bad, and incompetent.

A Shift Occurs

Other than those dynamics, my family life seemed basically ordinary and solid. My parents supported my siblings and me and encouraged us in our education. We took day trips as a family to various tourist sites around eastern Iowa. These were minivacations but also opportunities to see the "larger world" and learn. We laughed a lot around the dinner table and played softball and tag football in the yard together. I didn't sustain any major trauma in my early life. I remember being confident in school, having good friends, and being fairly good at sports. But when I was around ten years old, things began to change. I started to menstruate, years before most of my class-mates. I didn't feel comfortable talking about my experience with them. Menstruation was not ritualized and celebrated as an important milestone in my life as it is sometimes today. Mom just gave me a booklet to read on the subject. Other than that, she was silent. All in all, it wasn't a pleasant experience. I was often so sick during those times of the month that I would have to leave school and go to my grandmother's house in town to writhe in agony on her couch until my parents could pick us up after school. This whole experience caused me to doubt my body and therefore myself. My confidence and self-esteem began to slip away. I was becoming a woman, and that didn't seem like a good thing.

To make matters worse, my dad and I started growing apart. I had been his little buddy all my life, frequently follow-ing him around the farm and helping him with chores. Now I felt enshrouded in a dark mystery. No one talked about feel-ings, much less puberty, in my German family, but the silence spoke volumes. I began to feel that something was wrong with me. At the same time, I felt Dad pulling away, probably be-cause he had no idea how to treat a daughter who was now becoming a young woman. I no longer felt special.

Adding to my feelings of not being good enough was the fact that our old German Catholic pastor seemed consumed with preaching on sin, especially sexual sin, not a helpful focus for kids who were emerging as sexual beings. He would come into our high school classroom every year to talk about the Ten Commandments. But one odd thing (among many odd things) was that he never got beyond the sixth commandment (the seventh in the Protestant version of the Ten Commandments): "Thou shall not commit adultery." Not that any of us were in-clined to commit adultery. But we got the implied message—sexual sin was the worst sin, and girls were the main offenders.

We young people weren't empowered to claim the goodness

within us. On the contrary, it was emphasized that we were sinners—period. To be saved, we had to look outside ourselves to church authorities and the laws of the church to tell us what was real and good, but even more so to tell us what was sinful. On one hand, this view strengthened my reliance on God and the church, but on the other hand, it gave me the message that somehow God viewed me as flawed. Instead of seeing myself as a loved creature of God, all I saw was an unworthy creature of sin.

Overwhelmed by Shame

An example might help you see this misery as I experienced it. I was ten or eleven years old at the time. My younger siblings and I were playing in Grandma's yard in town, waiting for our parents to return. That particular day, the grandchildren of my grandma's next-door neighbor were visiting from far away. They wandered over into Grandma's yard, and we started playing together. Then, in a very unusual move for me, since I was basically shy, I decided it might be nice to ask Grandma to make some lemonade for all of us, since it was a hot day. It was a natural instinct, and I acted upon it.

Grandma's initial response was a long, ponderous sigh. I honestly don't know what Grandma was feeling or experiencing that day, but as kids do, I interpreted her response from my point of view. I read her sigh to mean, "How dare you put another burden on me today." I felt hurt, and soon that feeling moved to guilt and then to shame. I instantly realized that asking her for that favor had been a mistake, but not *just* a mistake. I judged my natural instinct as a selfish act. I saw myself as a bad person.

I don't remember if Grandma made the lemonade, but I do recall that every night, for weeks afterward, I berated myself for adding to her burden when she had so many other things to do. (This was similar to how I felt in relation to my mother.) I would lie awake at night crying, feeling like such a bad and selfish person for imposing on my grandma and making her life harder than it was. I couldn't see any way out of my misery. Perversely, I kept reminding myself of the incident, somehow thinking that if I suffered enough, maybe it would make up for my having caused Grandma to suffer. Through the years, this scene became almost a shame metanarrative for me, a story that resurfaced in my mind whenever I felt "less than" or "bad."

Although at the time I couldn't have named it, I have since come to understand—from my inner work in therapy and through my pastoral counseling training—that I was engulfed in shame. I began to study shame in order to get a fuller picture of the shame I was still enduring and discover how to heal from it. I learned that shame is the inner sense of feeling flawed or insufficient as a person. It involves seeing oneself as an oddity, and therefore exposed and vulnerable. Shame is often confused with guilt, but the two feelings are quite different. Guilt is about *doing* something wrong; shame is about *being* wrong. Guilt is about morality, while shame is about acceptability. With guilt, one can make amends, and there is hope. But with shame, there seems to be no solution except nonexistence, because shame is about the self.

Both women and men experience shame. However, the triggers and how it manifests itself are different for women and men. Brené Brown, a research professor at the University of Houston and one of the leading researchers and authors on shame and vulnerability, explores this in her book *I Thought It Was Just Me (But It Isn't): Making the Journey from "What Will People Think?" to "I Am Enough."*

> [W]omen experience shame as a web
> of layered, conflicting, and competing

> social-community expectations that dictate
> who we should be, what we should be, and
> how we should be. When I spoke with men,
> I didn't hear about layered, conflicting, and
> competing social-community expectations.
> The expectation, clear and simple: Do not let
> people see anything that can be perceived as
> weakness. (280)

As Brown suggests, women live with complex layers of expectations that they have internalized. I certainly did. For example, one expectation I lived with growing up was that my siblings and I shouldn't ever show that we were needy, so from early childhood on, I berated myself as being selfish if I expressed my needs. We weren't supposed to express negative feelings, so whenever I was hurt and cried, I was ashamed. I usually found my body too fat, not tall or pretty enough according to societal expectations. As I grew into adolescence, I kept comparing myself to other girls, and usually came up short. I found myself constantly on alert for what I "should" do. The stories I told myself reinforced the shame. Something in me seemed to be missing.

New Community, New Expectations, Same Old Shame

I brought this hidden shame with me as I entered my religious community, the Franciscan Sisters of Perpetual Adoration (FSPA), right out of high school.

The congregation was founded in Milwaukee, Wisconsin, in 1849. At first, the main ministries of the sisters were teaching, nursing, and caring for orphans among the German immigrants. Then in 1878, when there were more sisters, FSPA instituted a night and day prayer for the world called Perpetual

Adoration. Gradually, FSPA added new ministries, as the needs of the world dictated: works that included religious education, justice and peace ministries, missionary endeavors, and various diverse ministries across the United States, and in other places including China, Guam, and El Salvador.

The FSPA sisters had taught me throughout school, and I felt drawn to them because of the joy, hope, caring, and deep spirituality many of them exhibited. I also had two aunts in the community, so it was familiar to me, and I felt blessed to enter a community of sisters whose history showed them to be strong, courageous, forward-looking, and resilient women.

I don't really remember why I thought I had a vocation to religious life. But as I look back now, I think I knew that I wanted a college education, longed to move out of my small rural community to see and engage the larger world, and felt the strong desire to deepen my relationship with God. I think I was looking for a new life. Opting for religious life seemed exciting and hopeful.

The community welcomed me and supported me. I felt energized. I enjoyed my community life and became a good elementary school teacher, eventually teaching grades three through eight in the cities of Cedar Rapids, West Point, and Bellevue, all within a couple hours of my hometown of New Vienna.

Ironically, though, in becoming a religious sister, I had assumed another load of expectations from others—this time about who a sister should be, how she should act, and what she should say. I entered the community in 1967, right after the Second Vatican Council. This was a time of great change for the Catholic Church and therefore for the sisters in religious life. The council in effect flung open the windows of what had become a stuffy institution and engaged in the world. As a result, our incoming class in the convent became the first group to wear colored regular clothes instead of veils and habits.

Formerly strict rules were relaxed, and we were allowed to associate with laypeople much more.

Many Catholics and others saw the changes in sisters' appearances and behavior, and often didn't like it because, in nostalgic terms, they saw us as abandoning what "real sisters" *should* be like. I remember some of my aunts ruing the fact that I didn't wear a veil and habit. It just didn't appear "seemly" to them. These are funny examples of interactions that were mildly irritating to me. But it also was easy for me as one prone to shame to slip back into it, to see myself as not being good enough in other people's eyes.

A Crack in the Shame Wall

Throughout my twenties and thirties, I lived with this depleted sense of self. As a teacher and a community member, I was outwardly a success. But inwardly I felt like a fraud. I began therapy, which proved helpful at first. But I still felt like I was being judged by the therapist. I think this was partly due to my shame overwhelming me and partly because I was engaging in what was the wrong kind of therapy for me at the time, with too much emphasis on goals and expectations and not enough on mirroring the goodness inside me. I was still looking outward for approval.

Then one day I got angry, probably because of my lack of progress, although I'm not sure, because expressing anger wasn't something I did. Whatever the reason, that day I realized, *Something is wrong! I should be starting to feel better about myself!* I can best describe this feeling by using language that the feminist theologian and Sister of St. Joseph Elizabeth A. Johnson uses in her book *She Who Is: The Mystery of God in Feminist Theological Discourse*: "The judgment arises: we are worth more than this." (63) The inner voice that Johnson calls the "yes" in my being indeed rose up and said, "I'm worth more than this." This was pure grace!

Serendipitously, just when I needed help the most, my religious community was coming to realize the importance of mental health counseling for FSPA sisters who needed it. In 1983, FSPA founded the Franciscan Center for Wholistic Living in Saint Paul, Minnesota, which was open to women religious from any congregation. The program featured prayer, individual and group therapy, and classes in spirituality, exercise, healthy eating, learning to love the female body, art, journaling, and much more. I embraced this as a wonderful opportunity to address my shame issues. I entered the program in 1984 for a year, and that became for me the beginning of a whole new life, one in which I learned to love myself and become more of who I really am. I am forever grateful.

The key encounter during my time there happened fairly early in the process. I was seated in my therapist Jim's office. He was listening very attentively, as usual, but not saying much, also as usual. I was going around and around in an endless loop of questioning what I was going to do about something or other.

Finally, irritated with him for not helping me and feeling desperate, I confronted him. "Why don't you just tell me what to do?"

He calmly replied, "How can I tell you what to do? I'm not you. The answer is within you."

Trusting My Inner Voice

It didn't hit me fully right away, but what he said deeply challenged what I had been taught previously: that I needed to depend on a higher authority to tell me what to do. Jim was telling me to trust myself. The impact of his words has stayed with me all these years. They have led me to understand a powerful truth: Deep down, I have an inner voice, and I can trust it.

Thus began a search for confirmation of my basic goodness, a journey that would continue for many years. This process involved seeing a whole series of therapists and spiritual directors who saw the goodness in me, reflected it back to me, and accompanied me as I learned to claim it for myself. I also began studying women's psychology and feminist theology to find theorists (a number of whom I name in the next chapter) who resonated with my experience and placed it in a larger context, thereby offering explanations for my feelings and thoughts.

Through this process I learned, or learned again, many things that made sense to me. For example, God really is not a male. I knew that. So why does the church almost exclusively refer to God as "he"? I also knew that women were very scarce in the Bible, but I never recognized that, of the ones actually in the Bible, most are not named (e.g., the Samaritan woman, the bent-over woman, the woman with a hemorrhage). Why, then, do even minor male characters like Zacchaeus get named? Also, I learned that women can and should express anger, contrary to the teaching of society. I began to feel like I wasn't alone. I could now see that much of my shame resulted from the way that the church and society have excluded women and made them feel "less than."

All of this contributed to my emotional healing and growth. Gradually, through therapy, I was finally able to view and understand "my grandma scene" metanarrative from a more adult perspective. I realized that I had acted out of goodness and hospitality in asking for lemonade, and that Grandma's response was not my burden, but rather a reflection of where she found herself in her own life. I could finally forgive my ten-year-old self and even celebrate her for being kind and extending hospitality.

And still I continued to wonder how such a seemingly innocent interaction had caused me such pain and agony for so many years. What was underlying that pain? Why had it gained such a powerful hold on me?

During my long process of healing, I have shed many tears, asked lots of questions, and come close to despair. I have often felt very alone. But gradually I have also come to realize that many people have walked this same journey of healing ahead of me. I am beginning to sense their presence with me. This realization gives me hope.

2

Spiritual Authority

Deep down I have an inner voice, and I can trust it.

In those months at the Franciscan Center for Wholistic Living in Saint Paul, I learned that beneath my shame, I carry a powerful energy hidden within me—an inner voice. That voice is literally "goodness" personified. This truth is written in the Hebrew Scriptures: "This command that I am giving you today is not too wondrous or remote for you. It is not in the heavens. . . . Nor is it across the sea. . . . No, it is something very near to you, in your mouth and in your heart, to do it." (Deuteronomy 30:11–14)

Meggan Watterson, author, speaker, and Harvard-trained scholar of the divine feminine, writes about this inner voice in her book *Mary Magdalene Revealed: The First Apostle, Her Feminist Gospel and the Christianity We Haven't Tried Yet*. She states that this inner voice is our spiritual authority, which she defines as "the authority to tell the truth about our own story." (xiv) Watterson explains that women don't need anyone else to define who we are. We just need to get in touch with ourselves.

People have many different names for this phenomenon:

inner voice, true self, authentic self, the real you, soul, spiritual essence. I like the term "inner knowing" because a feeling of *knowing* is exactly what I get when I get in touch with my inner truth. I further resonate with the term "spiritual authority" to describe the power to speak this truth, which comes from God.

Souls Seeking God

There is a part of each of us that is pure good, from God, commonly known as the soul. As Scripture states, "God saw everything that [was created] and indeed, it was very good." (Genesis 1:31) That includes us. I believe our call in life is to manifest goodness, and to see goodness in all creation. I like to think of a "green thread" as an image of God's goodness, love, and grace constantly tying us all together through the centuries if we are willing to see and grasp it.

I believe that our souls are always seeking a connection with God, who is our true home, even when we are not aware of it. Too often I get distracted by all the noise around me—what are "they" saying, what is the "in" thing, what am I expected to do? But, as the psalmist says, "For God alone my soul waits in silence; for my hope is from God." (Psalm 62:5) When I engage in quiet reflection and contemplation, those noises quiet, and I dive into the Mystery within me, where I am able to recognize God's voice within and outside of me, in other people, in nature, in beauty, everywhere. At that moment, I feel at peace.

If we have done sufficient psychological, emotional, and spiritual healing work so that our inner filters are fairly clear, we will be able to recognize the reality of creation—that all are one, that we are good, and that we are loved. When we reach this point, shame no longer has the upper hand. James A. Houck Jr.—an ordained elder in the United Methodist Church, a professor of pastoral counseling, and a licensed professional counselor—writes the following:

> Interestingly, when people fully embrace the fact that they are a soul, and are indeed precious in the eyes of God, the compassionate, nurturing side of humanity emerges in a powerful way. Issues of prejudice, sexism, egocentrism, racism, etc. all go out the window; these simply cannot dwell in the higher consciousness of the soul. (109)

Such people recognize with spiritual vision what is real and true, and are then able to proclaim it with spiritual authority.

Embracing Our Spiritual Authority

What I have just described is a revolutionary act. Revolutionary, because most of us don't tend to think of ourselves as having inner authority, much less the authority to teach or preach. I know I didn't. In my mind, inner authority was the purview of theologically educated men. Wasn't it?

But here is what I did not yet fully grasp: Jesus was revolutionary! Although he was a poor, uneducated carpenter's son, he stood up to speak in the temple. What audacity! Yet he had heard and recognized God's voice within, and felt compelled to proclaim it.

People were utterly amazed when he did. As the Christian Scripture recalls, "[W]hen the Sabbath came, [Jesus] entered the synagogue and taught. They were astounded at his teaching, for he taught them as one having authority, and not as the scribes." (Mark 1:21–22)

Christianity has always believed that Jesus had spiritual

authority that came directly from God. Other religions believe that their founders, too, had spiritual authority. I cannot speak from experience in those religions. I can personally attest, however, that Christianity has not been very good at passing on the message to ordinary people that we, too, have spiritual authority, and we all have the responsibility to use it wisely.

In fact, quite the opposite is true: We as a people (both within and outside of Christianity) have been led to believe that only men such as theologians, priests, ministers, rabbis, imams, and so forth have spiritual authority, because they are the ones who have studied the scriptures and learned theology in school. Never mind that women were excluded from those schools and from those opportunities. The implication is that women wouldn't know what to do with the truth. We are told that for our salvation we have to listen to these ordained men who have all the answers.

From the point when laypeople first had access to Bibles, which occurred when the printing press was invented in the middle of the fifteenth century, until after the Second Vatican Council in the 1960s, private reading of the Bible was often not encouraged by the Catholic Church, because the hierarchy believed that people might go astray without the benefit of biblical interpretation by the clerics. That explains why my family had a beautiful old Bible displayed in our house, but no one ever read it. It just served as a repository for birth and death records of family members. How sad! We missed out on a lot.

Scripture tells us, though, that Jesus gave his followers spiritual authority. Consider the following verse: "Then Jesus summoned his twelve disciples and gave them authority over unclean spirits, to cast them out, and to cure every disease and every sickness. . . . These twelve Jesus sent out . . . to proclaim the good news, 'The kingdom of heaven has come near.'" (Matthew 10:1, 5, 7) All of us have been given spiritual authority to proclaim the good news. It is both a privilege and an obligation. No one is exempt. Meggan Watterson explains.

> Spiritual authority cannot be determined by a person's sex, gender, or sexuality but rather by the depth of their spiritual transformation and subsequent wholeness. Meaning, a person attains the spiritual authority to speak about Christ, or to proclaim the "good news," not because of what they look like externally but because of how arduously they have worked internally at uniting the self with the soul. (76)

We have all been gifted by God with spiritual authority. What a shame it would be not to use it to make the world a better place.

Spiritual Authority and the Ego

Embracing our spiritual authority doesn't mean that we can do and say anything we feel like, with no consideration of others or of nature. As Watterson states above, spiritual authority must be cultivated. It requires opening our minds and hearts to God, others, and the rest of creation, in addition to ourselves, in order to find the wisdom within. In this process, we might consult Scripture, tradition, wise teachers, our own experience and that of others for further input. In the end, we must be still in order to recognize the voice of the Spirit within us. Once we hear that voice, we must speak it aloud. Every morning, I pray this prayer: "O Lord, open my lips, and my mouth will proclaim your praise."

The effects that result from our actions point to whether we are speaking out of our spiritual authority or out of our ego.

According to Scripture, this list of outcomes—called the gifts or fruits of the Holy Spirit—will help us to discern whether our actions are of the Spirit: love, joy, peace, patience, kindness, goodness, faithfulness, gentleness, and self-control. (Galatians 5:22–23) If what we are saying and doing does not produce these fruits, then we are not claiming our spiritual authority.

For many women, it is not an abundance of ego but rather an absence of ego that gets in the way. Women especially have a hard time claiming spiritual authority. We often don't feel worthy, in general. Our agency, or power to act in the world, has too often not been recognized, and too often it is even demeaned. We might hear, "What do you know of spiritual things?" And if we think we do know about spiritual things, we are frequently told in not-so-subtle ways by men, and sometimes even women, that we don't know what we're talking about.

Rebecca Solnit, historian, activist, and author of more than twenty books, explains in her book of essays, *Men Explain Things to Me*, how this disproportionate tendency to challenge women's expertise chips away at women's confidence.

> Every woman knows what I'm talking about.
> It's the presumption that makes it hard, at
> times, for any woman in any field; that keeps
> women from speaking up and from being
> heard when they dare; that crushes young
> women into silence by indicating, the way
> harassment does, that this is not their world.
> It trains us in self-doubt and self-limitation
> just as it exercises men's unsupported over-
> confidence. (4)

What about you? Do you fear speaking with spiritual au-thority? Do you hear yourself saying or thinking things like "I can't speak at this meeting because I have different opinions and feelings than everyone else? They'll never believe me!" Or "I'm seen as a second-class citizen, and so my truth doesn't seem to matter." Or "My mother and the church itself taught me to be a good little girl, to stay in the background, and to not let my voice be heard." All this self-talk demeans our spiritual authority. However, once we women do claim our spiritual authority, we can't hold it in. The Spirit of Jesus moves in us with the breath of life.

New Ideas, New Ways of Being

As I approached midlife, I was no longer willing to deny the inner voice that was my spiritual authority. It had become too important to me. A key milestone in claiming my true self came out of my experience in the 1980s in Oklahoma City, where I had gone to take on the ministry of principal of a Catholic elementary school. Instinctively, I had chosen this new place far away from Iowa and Wisconsin, where I had been based before. I say "instinctively" because somehow I knew that in order to embrace my new life and inner freedom, I needed to live in a place where I wasn't overwhelmed with old expectations. Looking back, I think my inner voice and spiritual authority had revealed themselves to me, and I followed them.

During my years in Oklahoma City, I risked going outside the "usual" religious narratives I had heard my whole life. I knew there had to be more; my newfound healing and wholeness demanded more. I began to explore theology written from the underside, from those we don't normally believe can do theology—the poor, people of color, laypeople, non-Europeans, and yes, women too. I especially read Christian feminist theologians like Rosemary Radford Ruether, Elizabeth A. Johnson, and Elisabeth Schüssler Fiorenza, and women's historians like

Gerda Lerner, who wrote on patriarchy. They inspired me and opened up a world broader and deeper than the one that only white male clerics kept telling me about. They described other aspects of God, and myself, that I hadn't understood before: that God wasn't male or female, that God loved me, that I was good, that sin did not need to define me.

It was in this environment that I started experimenting with some of the "rules" with which I had been raised. One example is Good Friday. Previously, I had always experienced that day as a time for me to double down on my view of myself as a sinner. After all, I had been taught that Jesus died for me because I was bad.

But, in my third year in Oklahoma, instead of going to Good Friday services, I went to *Dead Man Walking*, the movie based on the bestselling book by Sister Helen Prejean, about her visits to a man on death row. Skipping Good Friday services seemed like a bit of a risk to my spiritual well-being. At least, I could imagine being told that it was. But in the theater that day, I experienced the deep tenderness and compassion Sister Helen gave to a condemned murderer, modeling the compassion that Jesus showed to his fellow condemned men on the cross. This reinforced for me that I, too, am loved and good, and that my call is not to focus on my sinfulness but rather to be more like Jesus: to actively love and bring compassion to all I meet, no matter the consequences. I felt renewed. Good Friday rituals in the past had never inspired me that way.

Some of my sisters in community at that time were also actively pursuing feminist ideas and theology. When we got together at meetings in La Crosse or elsewhere, we would share ideas and often create prayer services that contained this theology of a loving God. These brave, creative women were an energizing force for me. They often faced resistance to these new ideas, like scoffing or expressions of mistrust, from both inside and outside the community, but they kept walking the path of growth. I even was able to claim my femininity to a greater extent than I had before. I remember buying a pair of long, dangling earrings for the first time. They became a symbol for me that I was a woman, and a beautiful one at that.

Simply Karen

Since there were only a few sisters from my community in Oklahoma, I made many friends among the laypeople in the parish. Some are still good friends to this day. This opportunity freed me to be simply Karen, rather than having my identity focus mainly on being a religious sister. And these friends kept it real for me, then and now. I wasn't put on a pedestal; I was one with them. Too much so, maybe, since they felt no inhibitions about shouting for me to run faster as I rounded the bases in my Orange Crush T-shirt during our interparish softball games! And I certainly had no hesitation razzing them back.

I recall another grace-filled experience in Oklahoma that happened during a school board retreat. The facilitator asked those of us present to answer this question: "What are you passionate about?" This question sent an electric current through my body. The first thought that came to me was *Not being a principal*. I was shocked that it came through so clearly, but it felt right. I wasn't passionate about being a principal. And, in that moment, I realized that it was important to me that I be passionate about whatever ministry in which I was engaged. I didn't want to just fill a slot. I needed to bring my whole self to it.

The next day after the retreat ended, with newfound energy, I went to the library and located a catalog from Loyola University Chicago, which offered a master's degree in pastoral counseling. I was thrilled! I was even more thrilled when my religious community approved my request to leave the principalship in Oklahoma and sent me to study at Loyola for two years.

During my master's work at Loyola, and during my subsequent study for a doctor of ministry degree at Chicago Theological Seminary, I focused on women's psychology and spirituality around the issue of shame. I used my own story to ground me in the questions I explored.

My doctoral thesis was titled "And She Was Very Good," echoing God's words in Genesis 1:31. In it, I proposed a new methodology for pastoral counselors that focused on discovering and empowering the client's goodness and strengths rather than fixating on what was perceived to be wrong with him or her. Throughout the various ministries I've served in, both before and after my master's and doctoral work, I have spent my life looking for goodness, in myself, and in others.

Looking for Good, Doing the Work

One of my core beliefs is that people are all created basically good and remain basically good. As I have grown in the knowledge and experience of being loved by God, I have refused to believe in original sin anymore. I believe in original blessing. Sin was not original; being created good was the original act of God.

This idea is not a new one, nor is it unique to me. In 1995, Matthew Fox, now the author of thirty-eight books on culture and spirituality, wrote *Original Blessing: A Primer in Creation Spirituality*. Reading this book had a powerful effect on me, and I have believed in this principle ever since, even when the church seemed to have a problem with it. I believe that even when we sin and go astray, the spark of the Divine remains central to our being and constantly yearns for unity with God.

This process of claiming and expressing the spark of the Divine within me will be a lifelong journey. It may be for you as well. This work doesn't come easily, because there are often many forces lined up against us. Many of us have tried to be "good little girls and boys" our whole lives, going along with the system, never speaking out, so that we could be safe and okay. But I could do this no longer.

Now that I've come alive and am more in touch with my own spiritual authority, I realize that it is not enough for individuals like me to focus solely on our own healing. Our individual healing is necessary, of course, but our entire earth community is crying out for healing.

I believe that we all need to get involved. None of us does it alone. I believe it's important for us to go against the individualism of our culture and walk with others who seek to make the world a better place. They are waiting for us, even when we are not aware that they are.

3

What Has Taken Us So Long?

By the time I set out to explore how my family's history had impacted my life, I had done inner healing and worked on my shame issues for many years. I had learned to speak up in meetings and in other interactions. But the challenge of speaking one's truth for the sake of justice goes beyond the personal. This can be a difficult concept for white Western women to embrace, in part because we have been thoroughly steeped in a culture of individualism. But especially now in the twenty-first century, with the influence of social media, we can't help but see that we are part of a much larger milieu.

It is true that we all have many expectations put on us, starting with our families and spiraling outward. As individuals, we were born to parents who had already been shaped by their own families of origin, and who had possibly emerged with negative images of themselves and strong expectations of how they wanted their children to be better. Overt and covert messages like these often became the rule in families:

- Don't get angry.
- Don't cry.
- Don't ask questions.
- You're not good enough.
- You're too stupid.
- You're so fat.
- You'll never accomplish anything.

Maybe because of our Germanic heritage as well as what my parents had been taught, there was an expectation in our family that we were never to express strong feelings, except when they were happy ones. I didn't know what to do with feelings like anger, fear, sadness, and shame, so I tried to keep them in. But as they built up inside me, I would often start crying, for no apparent reason. Crying wasn't helpful in letting people know how I felt, but the tears just came. So, in effect, I made myself a victim instead of claiming my power to feel.

It's not unusual that I responded in this way. Since we as humans have an innate need to belong, we believe what our families tell us. But it's not just the message that trips us up; it's also how the message is delivered. People may communicate in a shaming manner, either vocally or through silence. Brené Brown makes an interesting observation in her book *I Thought It Was Just Me (But It Isn't)*.

> We can all recall experiences of feeling reject-
> ed, diminished and ridiculed. Eventually, we
> learned to fear these feelings. We learned how
> to change our behaviors, thinking and feelings
> to avoid feeling shame. In the process, we
> changed who we were and, in many instances,
> who we are now. (xxiv)

It is not just families that deliver messages and expectations that can lead to shame. These messages and expectations also come from our culture, media, advertising, education, politics, social media, religion, and many other places. Have you heard (outright or implied) messages like these?

- Real men don't cry.
- Beautiful women are thin.
- It's all in your head.
- Go back where you came from. You don't belong here.
- You're handicapped; don't attempt to be normal.
- Hide your sexual orientation.

I'm reminded of Twiggy, a fashion model from England in the 1960s, when I was a teen. She was stick-thin with no womanly curves, thus earning her the nickname. She became a cultural sensation, and the modeling and advertising realms put her forth as a physical template of how all girls should look. Clothes were designed around her body shape.

Well, I was not stick-thin and probably had no chance of ever looking like Twiggy. And that made me feel bad. Because of the cultural expectations, I hated how I looked and saw myself as flawed. Again, shame descended.

Our culture teaches us about shame. It mandates what is acceptable and what is not, who is acceptable and who is not. These negative messages seep into all of us. We accept them as truth. And the result is that we begin to think we have to hide our true selves, which is the real shame. In addition, we learn to mistrust each other's spiritual authority and to negatively judge each other for not living up to our culture's mandates.

Patriarchy and Misogyny

Rita Nakashima Brock, a Protestant feminist scholar, nonprofit director, and activist, and Rebecca Ann Parker, a theologian, activist, and former president of Starr King School for the Ministry, reflect on this phenomenon of negative judgment in their book.

> Western Christians are used to seeing human nature as sinful, weak, or flawed and to regard human nature in individual, rather than collective, terms. . . . Christ-likeness is found not in gaining power and using it but in abnegating it through surrender, obedience, and humility. (175–176)

I believe that one of the systemic problems in our Western culture that leads to shame is patriarchy, and another is its enforcement arm, called misogyny. Patriarchy is defined as the belief and practice that men have a natural right to rule over women, children, slaves, and property with unquestionable authority. Just to be clear, standing up to patriarchy isn't about man-hating. I know many men whom I like and admire who don't feel the need to lord their authority over others. What patriarchy refers to is not men but rather an institutional system that skews the natural balance, overemphasizes the traits often associated with the masculine, and rejects those traits often associated with the feminine and the natural world. When this inclination becomes outsized and perverted, domination and control become the modes of operation.

When patriarchy is threatened by women gaining too much power, then misogyny enters the picture. Misogyny was defined by the *Oxford English Dictionary* in 2024 as the "hatred or dislike of, or prejudice against women." But most men don't hate or have contempt for women. Misogyny is rather the system or environment where women face hostility and endure attempts to keep them subjugated.

I have seen misogyny play out in multiple systems—in government, business, education, the justice system, churches, culture at large. I have been appalled when news reports describe the demeaning of women who come forth to speak their truth in public, in court, or in Congress, painful though it may be. I remember how outraged I was with the treatment of Christine Blasey Ford in the Congressional confirmation hearings for Brett Kavanaugh for the Supreme Court in 2018. Ford, a distinguished professor of psychology at Stanford University Medical Center, came forward and accused Kavanaugh of having sexually assaulted her when she was in college, but a whole group of Congressmen treated her like a little girl who just didn't remember what happened. It was shameful! I was similarly appalled when some notable male figures in a number of our recent election cycles proclaimed that a woman couldn't be elected president. Rather than reacting in horror, most people said, "They're probably right." How sad!

Another obvious example of misogyny for me as a Catholic is the church's ongoing ban on ordaining women to the priesthood. I say that not because I want to be a priest. I don't. But many women do recognize priesthood as their call from God. The arguments used against priesthood for women, or really any kind of leadership of women in the church, are pretty ridiculous. Mary Jo McConahay, a prominent Catholic journalist and former war correspondent in Central America, rebuts several of these arguments in her book *Playing God: American Catholic Bishops and the Far Right*.

> [The response from the hierarchy is often that] the original twelve apostles were male, suggesting that this fact means females cannot succeed them as priests. . . . And Jesus was male, so a woman cannot "image" him. . . . The theological response held by

women who aspire to the diaconate and the
priesthood, and their male and female allies,
is that such thinking is heretical, because the
church teaches that the resurrected Christ is
God and, as every Catholic . . . learns, he or
she, male or female, disabled or in any other
way limited in life, is made in the "image of
God." (181)

Such so-called biblical arguments play a role in creating
and maintaining societies that are antagonistic to women in
leadership. In her fascinating book *The Authority Gap*, Mary
Ann Sieghart—a longtime, well-respected journalist, a BBC
Four presenter, and a professor at Oxford and King's College—
interviewed scores of women who are proven leaders in many
different venues, including politics, government, business, education, science, and journalism. The great majority of these
women reported that they continue to encounter challenges to
their leadership abilities and their authority because they are
women.

However much lip-service we pay to gender
equality these days, the authority gap still
looms large. Its covert bias can be just as dam-
aging, if not more so, than the old-fashioned
kind. These more subtle acts of discrimination
are much more frequent, and their effects ac-
cumulate quickly over time. Being interrupted,
ignored, challenged, talked over, undervalued
and underestimated . . . each could be called
a micro-aggression, but the macro-effect on
women is cumulatively as large as the traditional forms of bias, when women simply
weren't allowed to do certain jobs. (70)

Such treatment happens all the time, and that's why many people, including women, often fail to question it. Many explain it away, saying simply, "It's just how things are."

Listening to Our BIPOC Sisters

Patriarchy and the resulting misogyny have been given legitimacy through the laws enacted by the church and governments, through religious and political philosophies that undergird the thinking of nations and peoples, and through the stories our culture tells us about ourselves. And many of us, both women and men, but especially women, have kept quiet. I am sorry to admit that I, too, have kept quiet many times. It feels safer to just go along with the system, to not stir up the waters.

However, some of our Black, Indigenous, and People of Color (BIPOC) sisters have not remained silent. In her book *Women Who Run with the Wolves*, Clarissa Pinkola Estés, a Jungian analyst and first-generation American raised in the Mestiza Latina tradition (a combination of Spanish and Mexica or Native American), challenged women with these words:

> Many women are in recovery from their
> "Nice-Nice" complexes, wherein, no matter
> how they felt, no matter who assailed them,
> they responded so sweetly as to be practically
> fattening. Though they might have smiled
> kindly during the day, at night they gnashed
> their teeth . . . fighting for expression. (92)

Estés wrote that in 1992. More recently, writer Samantha Worley issued a new challenge in an article titled "Dear White Women: Here's Why It's Hard to Be Friends with You."

> White women are socialized to keep the
> status quo. They maintain patriarchy by
> "knowing their place" while at the same time
> relying on white supremacy to keep some
> sort of power. . . . White women's internalized
> misogyny and white supremacy cannot exist
> without each other. White women must con-
> front and dismantle both within themselves
> instead of projecting them onto Black women.
> (*An Injustice! Magazine*, April 2021)

That's a direct hit! I can recognize my behavior at times in the words of this quote. I feel guilty. But I now know that I don't have to feel shame. I know that I have the power to change. But first, I need to better understand what I'm dealing with.

Who Is In; Who Is Out

Patriarchy combined with misogyny, with white supremacy added in, makes a lethal cocktail. White supremacy results from patriarchy proclaiming who is acceptable and who isn't. Whole groups—people of color, immigrants, Indigenous people, women, the differently abled, older people, the LGBTQ+ community, non-Christians, and many others—have been deemed by our US culture to be "unacceptable" and thus marginalized. This systemic dualism or "either-or" thinking (acceptable vs. unacceptable) rewards the human over the rest of creation, white people over people of color, rich over poor, men over women, what's considered "normal" over what's considered "abnormal." The belief that "white" people or people with lighter skin are superior to those with darker skin leaves an indelible wound on persons not deemed "acceptable," while also opening them to oppression and violence.

To me and to many others, religious patriarchy is the worst kind of patriarchy as it is exercised in the name of God, and people are naturally afraid to disrespect God. Whenever religion and patriarchy are combined, the negative power of patriarchy increases a hundredfold. That is because religion speaks to our souls and deeply touches our sense of self. It addresses a tender place within us that can be easily and profoundly wounded if we are constantly told that we don't belong or we are not acceptable.

Thomas Aquinas, later proclaimed one of the foremost saints in the Catholic Church, taught in the thirteenth century that women were defective physically because men were the pinnacle of creation. Here is how Elizabeth A. Johnson interprets Aquinas's teaching in her book *She Who Is: The Mystery of God in Feminist Theological Discourse*.

> Since the soul informs the body, woman's defective physical state leads Aquinas to the conclusion that woman's soul is likewise deficient, her mind weak in reasoning, and her will fragile in choosing the good. For her own good, she needs to be governed by others wiser than herself. . . . From woman's natural inferiority in the order of creation, Aquinas reasonably deduces a host of consequences, such as . . . women may not be ordained priests since priesthood signifies the eminence of Christ and women do not signify what pertains to eminence; women should not preach since this is an exercise of wisdom and authority of which they are not capable; and so on. (24–25)

Do these arguments sound familiar? I have heard them stated or implied many times. And I am sure that my women ancestors lived under the pall of these same descriptions. When these types of judgments are heard often enough, women internalize the messages and come to believe them. Many women, including me, let notions and images like this seep into our psyches from childhood on. We believe that we are weak and powerless. And we are ashamed of this. In an earlier chapter, I explained that guilt is about *doing* something wrong; shame is about *being* wrong. Constantly being told in Christian churches that one's being is essentially wrong, that we are basically sinners, definitely leads to a sense of powerlessness and shame.

Shame, Again

Healing from shame is so difficult because shame counts on silence. Our individual silences lead in turn to an entire culture attempting to keep shame at bay. This inevitably leads to a sickness that permeates our public lives in destructive and insidious ways. These ways include depression, anxiety, addiction, bullying, sexual assault, and all types of violence.

As a therapist, I used to offer workshops on shame. Whenever these workshops were marketed as dealing with shame specifically, few people would register. But if the same topic was marketed differently, in terms like personal growth, then people would eagerly sign up. "Shame" was too shameful to talk about.

In the twentieth century, many people turned to the new discipline of psychology for help with their depression or anxiety. But in the beginning, traditional methods of psychology often increased feelings of shame, especially in women. Although for the most part this has changed, psychology in those early days tended to focus on inner pathology to the exclusion of relational and societal influences.

Women were told that the problem lay within them, that they were sick. Therapists often didn't listen *to* patients; they listened *for* their pathology. This kind of stigmatization focused on what was wrong with the person, not what was right, and therefore deepened their pathological shame while ignoring their strength and resilience.

Compounding the problem was the fact that the therapist was seen as the expert who knew it all and the patient as ignorant of the roots of her illness. Women who came into therapy already feeling helpless and powerless found that belief reinforced. And any confidence they may have had in their own spiritual authority was further quashed. I experienced this myself when I first began therapy, and it made me so ashamed, and then so angry. Does my experience resonate with you?

More and more these days, I have been thinking about my ancestors, about the women who came before me, who faced these same forces that were determined to separate us from our spiritual authority. I find myself identifying with voices from the past, those who lived in shame caused by both church and conquering powers.

What, I wonder, did they experience?

Were they able to heal from their shame?

"Moin."

*(Translation from Low German,
similar to Old Saxon: "Hello.")*

4

My Christian Foremothers

To risk speaking out of our spiritual authority, women need support and encouragement from companions and guides. We need to consider the question: Who has walked this journey ahead of me?

As you may remember, I was met with silence when I tried to learn about my ancestors. There simply wasn't enough information available to me to learn anything useful (or so I thought at the time). I did, however, know from my study of feminist Scripture scholars like Elisabeth Schüssler Fiorenza that there were women in the early church who claimed their spiritual authority. And so I turned first to these Christian foremothers.

Women in the Early Christian Church

Rita Nakashima Brock and Rebecca Ann Parker devote a whole section of their book *Saving Paradise* to this topic. They report that women in early Christian communities claimed their spiritual authority based on the belief that all humans can tap into the spark of the Divine within them.

> They regarded themselves as infused with the
> Spirit's power and restored to their freedom
> and dignity in paradise (191)

The Acts of the Apostles and Paul's letters in the Christian Scriptures show that women were very active in the early Christian community. Wealthy women, like Lydia, a dealer in purple cloth (mentioned in Acts 16:14–15), used their influence to support the new Christian movement. They opened their homes to serve as household churches where the Christians gathered. They welcomed roving disciples and preachers like Paul into their homes and provided them with what they needed. These more intimate interactions and relationships demonstrated the love and compassion of Jesus to Christians and non-Christians alike.

Women were able to do all this, even though they lived in a patriarchal environment ruled by the Romans, because the Christian movement itself valued women and other marginalized people as equal members of the community. In Paul's letter to the Galatians, he says, "There is no longer Jew or Greek, there is no longer slave or free, there is no longer male and female; for all of you are one in Christ Jesus." (Galatians 3:28) This was a radical stance, one that often led early Christians into conflict with the Pharisees, but that also enlivened and energized the early Christians and drew them together as one family.

According to Nakashima Brock and Parker, it is important to note that these women could also claim their spiritual authority because the beliefs of the Christian community at that time emphasized the resurrection of Jesus, not the death of Jesus. They believed that he was alive among all of them now through the Spirit. They believed they could hear Jesus's voice within them and had the power to boldly proclaim it. The focus then was not on sin and the need for redemption in the afterlife as it has been now for centuries. The focus was on paradise, both here on Earth and in the afterlife. It was both now and not yet. Christians were taught to relish paradise in the now and strive to embody it in their daily lives, in order to rejoice in paradise in the afterlife.

This early Christian emphasis on paradise led both men and women to see themselves as good, to experience God's voice within themselves, and to be emboldened to speak it. Each member of the community was valued, and their contributions were welcomed. They were urged to live as a spark of the Divine in the world.

The Gospel According to Mary

When I first read about the early Christian emphasis on paradise, resurrection, and the goodness of everyone, especially in the book by Nakashima Brock and Parker, I was overwhelmed with awe and gratitude. Finally! I had been waiting so long to find this life-giving Christian message that was for everyone, especially for women. To let go of my shame and remain a Christian, I needed to hear and read a new story, one in which women were not omitted or portrayed only as sinners, but were loved, seen as beautiful and strong, and had powerful roles in the community. And here it was! These early Christians lived within a story of resurrection and hope for life here on Earth.

One of the key women disciples of Jesus was Mary of Magdala, usually referred to as Mary Magdalene. A manuscript titled "The Gospel of Mary," discovered in 1896, reveals the importance of Mary Magdalene in the early Christian movement. Meggan Watterson says that this manuscript reveals that Mary had a special relationship with Jesus, and that the other disciples knew of her power. Mary was the disciple to whom Jesus appeared first after his Resurrection, and she was the one who first proclaimed that Resurrection to the other disciples. Recently, Pope Francis honored Mary Magdalene's spiritual authority by naming her "the Apostle to the Apostles."

Again according to Watterson, the most important message of Mary's gospel was that "we are inherently good." (20) I have come to understand that to Mary Magdalene, sin wasn't about wrong actions, but about forgetting the intrinsic goodness of our souls and acting out of that false notion. This is the message that I have spent my whole life trying to retrieve and put into action.

What Mary Magdalene proclaimed and taught had a real resonance with the common people. She developed a large following through the years. Many women in the twenty-first century have rediscovered Mary Magdalene as a model, giving them courage to claim their own power and spiritual authority.

Rediscovering What We've Lost

I can imagine what you might be thinking at this point. This is a whole new version of Mary Magdalene than the one we grew up with. In fact, she is known by many as the penitent prostitute, definitely a sinner who was powerless and demeaned. How in the world can she be considered an important disciple? How did the story change so much?

Watterson's book was a big help to me in understanding how we lost so much. Here are some of the highlights of what occurred. By the fourth century, the New Testament, as we know it today, was in the process of being codified. Church authorities saw the need for a unified version of Christianity

since various Christian communities viewed the Jesus movement differently and had produced manuscripts that exempli-
fied these differences. As Watterson relates, "There was also
the more practical question of authority. Who would have the
authority to tell the story?" (45)

In the process of codification, many books and fragments
of writing about Jesus, including the Gospel of Mary, the
Gospel of Thomas, and the Gospel of Philip, which all alluded
to Mary's special relationship with Jesus, were eliminated from
the "orthodox" version of the Bible. These unorthodox versions
of the Gospels were deemed heretical. In addition, anything
that confirmed and validated women's leadership in the early
church was also excluded.

For example, how did Mary Magdalene become the penitent prostitute? Watterson explains.

> Over the centuries, Christ [was portrayed
> by theologians in the West as] less and less
> human; he was depicted as chaste, monastic,
> purely divine, and Mary Magdalene underwent
> the inverse transformation. She became more
> and more human, more "sinful." (106–107)

Watterson goes on to say that Pope Gregory, in a homily
in the sixth century, "conflated Mary Magdalene as both the
unnamed 'sinner' in Luke 7 who anointed Christ's feet, and the
Mary of Luke 8 and Mark 16 who is freed of all her demons by
Christ. And then he interpreted these passages as confirming
that Mary's sinfulness had to do with her sexuality. . . . Finally,
in 1969 . . . the church officially corrected his mistake. . . ."
(107) But unfortunately, many a preacher and ordinary person
still describe Mary Magdalene as the penitent prostitute and
believe that's what she was, despite there being no evidence to
support this claim.

A Need for Balance

Thus began the systematic exclusion of women from positions of authority within the church. No longer were the voices of women valued. Spiritual authority was made to reside only in male clerics. No longer were traits like focus on the inner world, feeling, intuition, and relationality valued in the church. Now the only traits that seemed important were the outer world, the rational, action, and seeing the world in separate parts.

Ideally, both men and women have some qualities from each category, making them balanced, although a few qualities will probably be more prominent at any one time. Organizations or movements also need all of the above to function wholly. When one set of traits is almost entirely missing, which is what happened in the Middle Ages, often dysfunctional behaviors become dominant, behaviors in this case like lust for power, authoritarianism, rejection of emotions and relationality, and violent action. And because the church was so powerful in the Middle Ages, it influenced related entities like empires, governments, culture, work, society, health care, education, and relationships to also become unbalanced.

This lack of balance is reflected in humans' destruction of nature. According to Sharon Blackie, "It's no accident that this systematic suppression of the feminine has been accompanied down the centuries not only by the devaluation of all that is wild and instinctual in our own natures, but by the purposeful destruction of natural ecosystems. We long ago turned our backs on the planet which gives us life." (33)

This imbalance in our world, where humans have disparaged women and feminine qualities in general, has led to so much devastation that it seems irredeemable. But with God, nothing is irredeemable.

Looking to the Light

Now don't get me wrong. Christianity is resilient and has been able through the centuries to bring inspiration, healing, and love to the world, even in difficult times. This may be hard to recognize. But when one separates Christianity itself from its power and clerical structures, it's easier to see the ways in which it has been a light in the darkness.

For example, even as women were silenced by the church in the Middle Ages, and sometimes even sent to convents to keep them under control, these same women often rose above these strict structures to become internally free, powerful, and outspoken. They found strength and power in sisterhood. Women religious became spiritual guides for laypeople, and sometimes wrote spiritual tracts or even whole books. Granted, they often had to claim a male cleric as the author of their writing to get it accepted by church authorities. Nonetheless, these women were known for, and sought out for, their spiritual authority.

They've been there in our history all along—largely unseen and unknown. However, only recently have some of these brave women been brought into the light, to serve as examples for all of us. In my childhood, the only women named in the Catholic Church's litanies were those named as saints by the male hierarchy. This usually included Mary, the mother of Jesus, and many, many martyrs—bloody victim martyrs. Today women have begun adding to the list of strong saintly women, rightfully claiming their own story. They have asked many women saints to intercede for us, including Elizabeth of Judea, Mary Magdalene, Hildegard of Bingen, Joan of Arc, Clare of Assisi, Therese of Lisieux, Catherine of Siena, Teresa of Avila, and Elizabeth Seton, as well as other women not officially declared saints. We are surrounded and supported by a large cloud of witnesses, both alive and dead, who witness to the love of God for all and inspire us to live just and faithful Christian lives.

More recently, the work of Elizabeth A. Johnson, in her book *Friends of God and Prophets: A Feminist Theological Reading of the Communion of Saints*, has given women (and men) a more complete understanding of the traditional Catholic "Communion of Saints." Johnson points out the importance of not just naming people who have been excluded, but remembering all they brought to the world in their time and how they continue to inspire us today.

> In addition to searching for women whose
> names and stories are preserved, however
> partially, in the tradition, women call to mind
> the generations upon generations of women
> whose bold mettle, touched with the grace
> of the Spirit, created and bequeathed life,
> warmth, beauty, skill, artistry, justice, insight,
> and goodness to the world, and whose pain
> and degradation leave terrifying memories
> that awaken the will to resist. (156)

Now, as more and more women from the past are being remembered, it is our privilege and call to get to know them, tell others, and draw on their strength and courage as we bring our own goodness and spiritual authority to the world crying out for healing.

"Moin."

"Kannst du mi vehieren?"

(Translation from Low German,
similar to Old Saxon: "Hello. Can you hear me?")

5

My Familial Ancestors

It is difficult to find and tell the story of my heritage when so little information about my familial ancestors exists. Because of this, I discovered that I needed to supplement the research I had done through books and online information with what I could gather from my intuition, my dreams, my imagination, my prayer and contemplation, and my lived experience. Some people might scoff at this nonlinear thinking being considered research, but I can personally testify that I have come to new awareness, knowledge, and consciousness through these other valid ways of knowing.

James A. Houck Jr., an ordained elder in the Episcopal Church and professor of pastoral counseling, says this about the impulse to seek out these connections:

> [T]he time has come to not only discover
> our soul's voice, but also hear the cries of our
> ancestors; generations whose souls long to
> be healed from their trauma and released to

God. Their stories are not over just because
they are no longer physically with us. Indeed,
they have much to teach us not just in terms
of how they suffered and died, but rather how
they lived and loved. (xiv)

As I have already said, healing must begin, for all of us,
in our own histories and stories. This is something I learned
in my forays into history, feminist theology and psychology,
sociology, and genealogy. And so I return to my own history
and stories, in the hope that my doing so may inspire you to
delve into yours.

In order to claim this relationship, I realized, I needed to
"re-member" them, meaning "to bring them together again,"
in the long line of family. Thankfully, I have the skills I need in
order to do this work. That's because I am naturally a weaver—
not of cloth, but of ideas and experiences. There is nothing I
enjoy more than seeing how concepts and experiences can be
brought together to create something new. So, despite having
little information about my ancestors, I tried to piece together
what I could find, and see how my green thread of life and
hope was woven through history. Sharon Blackie describes
this weaving process beautifully.

Women are spinners and weavers; we are the
ones who spin the threads and weave them
into meaning and pattern. Like silkworms, we
create those threads out of our own substance,
pulling the strong, fine fibers out of our own
hearts and wombs. It's time to make some new
threads; time to strengthen the frayed wild
edges of our own being and then weave ourselves back into the fabric of our culture. (361)

I am not just a weaver of ideas and experiences. I am a weaver of family connections too.

Back to My German Roots

I can trace my personal family tree back to the late 1700s. Perhaps unusually, all of my great-great grandparents hailed from the same area, what is now northwest Germany, around the towns Oldenburg, Holdorf, Paderborn, Vechta, and Hanover. Their names were Christopher and Katherine, Christ and Margaretha, Wilhelm and Bernadina, John and Anna, Johann Heinrich and Maria Agnes, Anton and Angela, Johann Bernard and Catherine, and John Joseph and Gertrudis. As I mentioned earlier, they were farmers and farmers' wives, had large families, and lived near small towns scattered across the countryside. The land featured flat farmland, streams, open pastures, small hills, and oak and other trees.

An important beacon found in each of these towns was the steeple of the local Catholic church. Each one could be seen for miles, a testament to the faith of the townspeople and the network of like-minded congregations in the area. All of my great-great-grandparents, on both sides, were Catholic, and most lived within fifty miles of each other. As you can see, my ancestry, at least at that time, was quite homogeneous.

Europe in the 1840s and 1850s was engulfed in political, social, and economic chaos and change. The French Revolution in the late 1700s had kicked off a wave of revolutions that rolled across Europe. People everywhere wanted more individual liberty and freedom. Science was gaining strength and popularity, often challenging what the church had been and was still proclaiming. People were also struggling economically. For example, in the area around Oldenburg, the oldest son was often given the land, leaving the younger sons few prospects for earning a livelihood beyond joining the military. This increased German discontent and desire to emigrate.

The allure of the New World was strong. The United States was offering a fresh start and plenty of cheap, rich land for farming. Newspaper ads announced that US land was being offered for only $1.25 an acre. The US government needed hardworking families to settle the West and develop that virgin territory. Many of my ancestors heard the message and were among the people looking to the New World for freedom and a chance to begin again.

All of my great-great-grandparents emigrated with their families to the United States between the years 1845 and 1874. Some landed in New Orleans and moved up the Mississippi River to Iowa. Others entered the country at New York or Baltimore and traveled overland to Iowa, some stopping for a number of years in western Ohio where there was an established settlement of German Catholics. My ancestors then all headed to a settlement called New Vienna, Iowa, where they knew people from their hometowns who had previously settled there. Rev. F. W. Pape describes the environment in an entry in the 1906 atlas of Dubuque County, Iowa: "New Vienna is located . . . in a beautiful valley . . . twenty-six miles due west of Dubuque, . . . just on the outskirts of the once-beautiful woodland bordering that great river [the Mississippi]."

New Vienna, so named because of the Austrian bishops' support of Catholic migration to the American western frontier, had been first settled in 1843 by five families from the Oldenburg, Hanover, and Westphalia regions of the northwest Germanic lands. The settlers were all Catholic farmers who wanted to establish a German American Catholic settlement in an area conducive to farming.

Soon fourteen other families from the same three regions joined the first settlers in New Vienna. Within forty years, these German Catholic settlers had spread out over an area of twenty square miles, numbering eleven hundred families, and establishing other settlements. They built beautiful Catholic churches with towering steeples, still visible from miles away. I fondly remember driving into New Vienna from north or south and seeing this cathedral-like edifice dominating our little town. Very impressive!

This homogeneous situation remained virtually the same until the 1970s. For good or ill, my people lived in a bubble, as it were, with little diversity. Growing up in the 1950s and '60s, I never knew a person of color nor more than a few non-Catholics.

As I delved further into the mystery of my ancestors, I kept finding hints about who they were before 1700 and what they may have experienced. References in history books to northwest Germany in the Middle Ages revealed that the inhabitants of the region before AD 800 were Saxons. Since my family history was so homogeneous and my ancestors were solidly planted in northwest Germany, I've come to the conclusion that my long-ago ancestors were probably Saxons.

Who Were the Saxons?

When I began looking into my ancestry, all I knew about the Saxons was what I had read in history books—that they lived in the Middle Ages, were very warlike, and practiced paganism. These people couldn't have been my ancestors, could they? How ironic! In my Catholic grade school, we used to pray for pagan babies so they wouldn't go to hell. We even contributed our nickels and dimes in an effort to send missionaries to convert them. Now I wondered: Was I myself a pagan baby?

This new awareness was astounding! But further research confirmed that information about the Saxons in general is scarce, since nothing much remains about the Saxons written in their own words. Their culture and language were wiped out. What secondary sources we do have hint at a wider, forgotten history. But much of what is known is taken from the descriptions and opinions of their conquerors, the Romans and the Franks—a group of Germanic people who lived in what is now France.

Needless to say, their accounts often tended to be biased. So, once again, I was met with relative silence. However, in my research, I did gather valuable information from Robert Sass's book *Saxon Paganism for Today* and from Nakashima Brock and Parker's book *Saving Paradise: How Christianity Traded Love of This World for Crucifixion and Empire*.

In them, I learned that the Saxons were a group of tribal people who lived near the North Sea coast in what is now northwest Germany and the Netherlands. The state in modern-day Germany where most of these Saxons lived is now called Lower Saxony.

The first likely mention of them is found in Ptolemy's *Geographia*, written in the second century AD. The Saxons' origins are unknown, but many scholars argue that they migrated from the north (from present-day Denmark or Norway) or were born as the result of intermarriage with their Norse neighbors.

To confirm my relationship to the Saxons, I took a DNA test and learned that I am 58 percent northwest German, 37 percent Danish-Swedish, and the other 5 percent from England and northwest Europe. This all seems to fit my theory.

The Old Saxons were unique among neighboring tribes in that they had no king. They were organized as a federation of one hundred gaus or clans. Each year the federation held an assembly that somewhat resembled a democracy, with thirty-six representatives from each gau attending (twelve nobles, twelve free men, twelve peasants). They met at a grove of oak trees near Marklo, located in present-day Westphalia,

Germany. The assembly began by invoking their gods and goddesses for protection and abundance in the coming year. Then they would do legislative business, and finally, the nobles would draw lots to see who would be the leader of the federation that year if there was a war. It is said that this practice of drawing lots showed their trust in their gods to direct their well-being.

The Saxons worshipped many of their own gods and goddesses, who were similar to Norse gods and goddesses. The main god was Uuoden, and the main goddess was his wife, Fria. He had healing power and was seen as the divine ancestor of kings. She was portrayed as being very wise and having the gift of foresight. Nerthus/Erda (Mother Earth), a giant fertility goddess equated with peace, was widely worshipped among Germanic tribes, including the Saxons.

The Saxons worshipped these divine beings in woods, near streams, and in front of a sacred oak tree. They never built churches for their deities. In AD 98, Cornelius Tacitus, a Roman writer, noted in chapter 9 of his *Germania*: "The Germans do not think it in keeping with the divine majesty to confine gods within walls or to portray them in the likeness of any human countenance. Their holy places are the woods and groves, and they apply the names of the deities to that hidden presence that is seen only by the eye of reverence." (quoted in James C. Russell, 108–109)

The Saxons were known as fierce warriors and coastal raiders in addition to being farmers. They sought to expand their homeland and prevent other groups from taking theirs. For centuries, the Romans struggled with the Saxons on many geographical fronts.

After the collapse of the Western Roman Empire in the late fifth century, the Saxons continued to press westward and southward. Because of their constant raiding, the authorities in Britannia struck a bargain—they permitted some Saxons to settle in areas of Britannia as farmers in exchange for the Saxons' service as mercenaries to protect the Britons from incursion by other groups. Eventually, other Saxons invaded or migrated to the island of Great Britain. This group of people were eventually called Anglo-Saxons. This name distinguishes them from the continental Saxons, or Old Saxons, who remained in the area of northwest Germany and the Netherlands. My ancestors were probably among these "Old Saxons."

Breaking Through the Silence

All of this is interesting to me. But at this point, I'm still back to the silence. I may be pretty sure of my ancestry, but without a lot more information, it's difficult to sense a relationship between the Saxons and myself.

Laraine Herring, author, teacher, and workshop presenter with degrees in creative writing and counseling psychology, states this in her book *Writing Begins with the Breath: Embodying Your Authentic Voice:* "Writing unleashes the silenced voices." (87) She elaborates on this as follows:

> I thought about the silences of my grand-
> parents' generation. . . . I thought about the
> stories their bodies held. . . . Where do those
> stories go once the last shovelful of dirt falls
> around the casket? Into the roots of the
> trees in the cemeteries? Then into the air we
> breathe from the photosynthesis of the trees?
> And then—into the nostrils of the writer
> walking past one spring day who suddenly
> hears, without a doubt, the whispering of an
> old man from Poland, or a Native American

woman from Dakota Territory, in her ear.
And then this writer, if she listens, goes home,
picks up her pen, and a voice that isn't hers
moves the ink. (85)

So, I picked up my pen and wrote.

*I am sitting under my cherished "Grandmother Oak" tree, jour-
naling. I can imagine my ancestors speaking to me. As a matter
of fact, I have been receiving unspoken, internal nudges that tell
me I need to be open to the world of my ancestors. This place
under their favorite tree seemed like a good place to start.*

*It is a warm day with the sun high in the sky, dappling
the leaves and creating flashes of light like diamonds skipping
all around me. Insects and birds are flitting around, creating
background sounds of life and energy. I close my eyes and settle
into peace. I allow myself to sink deep into myself and be open
to whatever inspiration may flood my soul.*

"Kannst du mi vehieren?"

*I wake with a start. Sitting next to me on the grass under
the oak tree is a woman with rosy cheeks and beautiful green
eyes regarding me directly and thoughtfully. She looks to be
in her late twenties, dressed in a gray woolen tunic with her
reddish-blond hair woven into a long, thick plait hanging down
her back. She is of medium height, somewhat stout with sturdy
legs extending out from her tunic.*

*She asks again, in a Germanic dialect, "Kannst du mi
vehieren?"*

I stammer, "I can't understand what you are saying."

*And then, through the magic and mystery of imagination,
she replies in English, "I asked, 'Can you hear me?'" She goes on
to say, "I am Grünthrad, a Saxon woman of long ago and your
ancestor."*

*"I can't believe you are here!" Making an effort to contain
my excitement, I tell her my name and explain that I have been*

researching my ancestry. "I have discovered that all my great-great grandparents came from the same northern lands that belonged to your Saxon people many centuries ago. I am looking for connection to them."

Grünthrad replies, "I sensed that you were calling me. Because you are my descendant, I thought you might listen. I have a terrible story to tell, but no one wants to hear it."

She pauses. Then suddenly she becomes agitated and angry and shouts, "I have been roaming all over! I can't rest! I can't be at peace with our gods! I need someone to hear what happened, and to accept my sadness and anger so I can let them go. I need help!"

"I—I want to know your story," I stammer. "Our story. It may be hard for me, but I'll try to really listen to you."

"That is all I need for now." She sighs.

Both of us become silent. We have a lot to ponder.

Eventually, Grünthrad disappears.

6

My Through-Line

Imagining the voice of Grünthrad has helped me to feel more connected to my ancestors. James A. Houck Jr. offers this explanation:

> [V]arious personal experiences reveal that
> the dead do speak in many ways. In fact,
> they speak to us in our dreams, through our
> conditioned behaviors, attitudes, perceptions,
> thought processes, learned helplessness, work
> ethics, inter-personal relationships, phobias,
> addictions, etc., all handed down to us from
> one generation to another. (4)

Houck's words ring true to me. I am now convinced that I am a recipient of Saxon DNA. I am indeed a "pagan baby." Who I am has been determined in part by the DNA passed down from the long-ago Saxons. But DNA is not the whole story. As the above quote states, an individual's traits and characteristics are passed down through both nature and nurture. What we learn from our families, environments, and communal narratives also influence who we become. What does my family system reveal? What have I been told about who I am, what have I *not* been told, and what do I tell myself? And you? What have you been told, or *not* told, about your background?

As a twenty-first-century Saxon, am I able to feel what it was like for my distant ancestors and how they influenced me? Can I hear their voices whispering in my ear?

I remember a time in 1999 when I traveled with a friend. Both of us wanted to visit the places where our ancestors had originated in northwest Germany. We visited Münster in Westphalia, where she actually ran into a shopkeeper with her same family name. We also visited Vechta, where my father's great-grandparents and grandparents originated, and though I didn't find any relatives living there, when I went to the local cemetery, I felt like I was home in Iowa. In that cemetery so far away, the names on the graves matched the names on the graves in my hometown. At that moment, I knew that I, too, had come from Vechta. It was a powerful awakening!

Connections to the Saxons

As I continued to think about the connections between my ancestors in northwest Germany and myself, many similarities struck me. One similarity is the importance of farming for the people in both my home area and the home of the Saxons. As I found on the Britannica website, "Agriculture [today], the traditional mainstay of the local economy, remains more important in Lower Saxony than in most other German states, with farms producing wheat, rye, oats, potatoes, sugar beets, and dairy and beef cattle." My parents' farm, too, has a long history, having been in our family for over a hundred years. Farming remains an important occupation for people in my home area.

As I indicated earlier, the terrain and the flora around my hometown were quite similar to that in northwest Germany, or they were when the first settlers arrived and before many trees were cut down in Iowa in the 1950s and 1960s to make room for more farmland. The similarity of the environment was probably one of the reasons these settlers from Germany were attracted there.

My brothers, Leon and David, who are much more sensate than I, reminded me of what our farm looked like when we were kids. According to them, most of the trees in the creek pasture and along the road were oak trees and poplars. Of the oaks, burr oaks predominated, but there were also pin oak, black oak, and white oak, and maybe red oak. In the two areas of woods on our farm, other trees included hackberry, ash, walnut, box elder, cherry, and maple.

Just like the original landscape in northwest Germany, the original landscape in northeastern Iowa featured oak savannas. A savanna is a mixed woodland-grassland ecosystem where trees grow far enough apart to allow the land beneath the canopy to remain open. As a result of this clearing, oaks in a savanna can grow taller and spread out more than in an oak woodland. The open canopy allows other vegetation and grasses to grow beneath it, which in turn provide food for animals, birds, and insects.

As I indicated earlier, many of the oak savannas were cut down by the earlier settlers. However, there are efforts now underway to restore this vibrant ecosystem.

Humans and Oaks

Oaks have been an important tree in the northern world for a long, long time. James Canton, lecturer and director of Wild Writing at the University of Essex, and author of the book *The*

Oak Papers, informs us that "the history of human existence across the northern hemisphere is tightly tied to oaks." (20) He then elaborates as follows:

> They gave wood for the fire, but their trunks could also be worked to form the frames of the homes that sprung up on the freshly cleared ground. And oaks offered more than merely wood. They gave acorns that could easily be gathered and stored and later eaten so that both humans and animals could feed and stave off starvation in times of famine. (21)

These mighty trees have long been important to humans in other ways as well as practical ones. In fact, oaks have served as spiritual symbols throughout the centuries. Because of their huge mass, stability, strength, long life, and ability to provide shelter and food for diverse species, many peoples considered the oak a symbol of the Divine.

Canton continues, "From the earliest Stone Ages through to the start of the Industrial Age merely a few hundred years ago, we have been dependent upon oaks and infused with worship of those trees, and religious practices centered on the most esteemed of the oaks that lay within our communities." (59) This is in line with the religious practices of the Saxons. Oak trees have always been considered very special, and even today really old ones are frequently called Grandmother Oaks.

The Oak Tree and Me

I have my own spiritual connection to an oak tree. Right outside my window in my former apartment, there was a beautiful large oak. It was so close that its branches overhung my balcony. It definitely was a presence! Every morning, I would sit in my comfortable chair in front of the window to pray, and I would look out at my oak tree, watch the leaves sway in the breeze and change colors through the seasons, delight in the squirrels chasing each other and leaping from branch to branch, spy birds flitting about, and hear their delightful trills. This was a place of stillness for me, a place of contemplation and mystery. The oak was a constant in my life, symbolizing strength, stability, vitality, and presence.

I have been delighted to hear that others also prayed with oak trees. A few years ago, I read an article by a Dubuque, Iowa, Franciscan, Sister Kathy Knipper, whose ancestors also came from Saxon lands. In her article "The Gift of Ancestral Rootedness," she reveals the following:

> When I need to discern and seek courage, I make my way to Grandmother Oak, a sprawling, ancient tree in the woods of the Midwest, and I sit with her grandeur. . . . Even though invisible, her roots are deep and wide, providing foundation to support change, transition, and fullness of life. She holds me in the embrace of life, energy flowing through her limbs. Even in the storms of life, vitality pulses. Her mighty branches are vulnerable to the elements, yet strong. Large, gnarled, graceful branches bless my being. They hold the mystery of changing seasons, reminding me of the great cosmic circle of life.

This connection between nature and spirituality is another similarity I share with earlier Saxons. As a child, I would often walk out to the creek pasture and enter a special place. There was an outcropping of large rocks on a hillside surrounded by trees above the stream. It created a somewhat closed-in area that I used as a "house," a place where I could sit and think and daydream and be totally myself. This was a spiritual place for me, although at the time, I wouldn't have been able to name it that way. We had been taught to identify spirituality with the church, the written word, and doctrine. But somehow deep down, I knew it was more than that.

In my small town of only three hundred people, we have a huge cathedral-like church whose grandeur is something to behold. But somehow the most meaningful moments in the church for me were often not the rituals held therein. It was actually the times when I had the church to myself. I could sit in a pew in the midst of mystery. I felt God's presence in the silence. I wanted to continue to feel loved, to love, and abide in this mystery. Maybe that was the beginning of my religious vocation.

I wonder if my father also experienced spiritual moments as he was riding on his tractor in the fields, going up and down the rows, plowing or harrowing or planting. Tractors back then weren't like they are now, with hermetically enclosed cabs, air-conditioning, radios, and plush seats. No, then tractors were simple and wide open to the elements.

So, as Dad would go back and forth for hours, he could feel the breeze, the warmth of the sun, the smells of the earth and the clover. And in that back-and-forth, back-and-forth, he would have been able to let his mind and heart wander and wonder, what we today might call meditation or contemplation. Like the Saxons, he personally recognized the sacredness of nature, and I could see that he was filled with peace and awe in the midst of it.

Speaking and Living Like a Saxon

Another similarity between my family and our ancestors is our native language. The Saxons' language, Old Saxon, is mostly lost to history, but linguists say that the closest remaining language to Old Saxon is "Plattdeutsch" or "Low German," still spoken in northwest Germany. As Britannica's website tells me, "The population of Lower Saxony regards itself as Low German, linked by a common ancient Saxon origin and the use of the Low German dialect. The latter, a dialect closely related to Dutch, Frisian, and English, is quite distinct from the official High German. Some regional literature is still written in this dialect."

My grandparents spoke Low German, along with English, as did the rest of the elders in my hometown from the time of their emigration until the 1950s and 1960s. My parents' generation spoke English, but they knew enough Low German to use it to keep secrets from us kids. I don't think it's a stretch to imagine that the language my grandparents still spoke was very similar to the language of my Saxon ancestors.

Still another similarity between the Saxons and my family is the need to freely live their lives. As you may remember, the Old Saxons did not have a king and operated with a system similar to a democracy. As a group of clans, they were fiercely independent. Iowa farmers are also quite independent. They really answer to no one, and often chafe under government interference.

These are just some of the common bonds I feel between myself and my Saxon ancestors. I can imagine myself as one of them, because I am. Can you imagine being one of your ancestors?

Miriam Therese Winter, a Medical Mission sister, author of numerous books on feminist and quantum spirituality, and singer and composer of sacred songs, conveys the idea of ancestral connections in her book *Paradoxology: Spirituality in a Quantum Universe*.

> It is said that remnants of our evolving are
> encoded in our DNA, that a long-forgotten

lineage lingers on in our cellular memory and
is transmitted in perpetuity from one generation to the next. Was it I who, once upon a
time, ran through forests, foraged for food,
and drummed and danced in the moonlight?
Did I fly through the wind currents effortlessly,
once upon a morning star, long, long ago? (26)

If all this is true, then we are indeed more connected to
our ancestors than we know. This realization feeds my practice of sitting with my ancestor. I imagine Grünthrad and her
people, glimpsing them in the sun and the moonlight. And I
picture them facing harder things.

Once again, I am sitting beneath my precious oak tree. Once again, I am engaging my imagination in the hope that Grünthrad will reappear. And she does!

"Moin, moin," she says in her Low German dialect. "I was reading over your shoulder when you didn't even notice me. I saw what you wrote about all the similarities between us. It is remarkable!"

"Yes, I found quite a few. It seems that much of you has passed on to me through the centuries." I briefly pause and then say, "You have a beautiful name. What does it mean?"

Grünthrad smiles as she answers. "My name means 'green thread' in my language. It is a way of honoring the greening of life in me. My mother always told me how strong and good I was. To remind me of this truth, she dyed a thread green and used it to sew my tunic together. Every time I dressed in the morning, I saw the green thread and remembered her words."

"Your mother was very wise."

"Ja, she was." After a pause, Grünthrad goes on. "I was partnered with a wonderful man named Odullieb, and together we had a strong and beautiful daughter named Läwen, which means life. Odullieb was a farmer, but in dangerous times he went off with the other men to protect our homeland. I hated those times! I worried that Odullieb would get hurt or would not come home at all." A dark gloom settles over her. "When he did come home, his eyes were filled with sadness and a deep haunting. And many times, he would get very angry. I was scared." She pauses, looking away for a moment. "It always took him a while to recover from the fighting."

Gathering herself, she continues, "I have always prayed to Mother Earth, who gives me solace. She is a good mother, so big and strong. She loves peace and makes everything grow. Every day, when I could get away, I would try to visit the old oak tree by the stream. It was so beautiful there. I lay down in the tall grasses with the sun warming me, listening to the sounds of the birds and the running water. There I felt the presence of my mother, holding me in her loving arms."

I can easily picture the scene she is describing. So I tell her I, too, have felt that same kinship with Mother Earth.

Grünthrad smiles and continues her story. "Besides my other duties, I was also a healer. My mother taught me to recognize both healing and dangerous plants. I was already teaching the same things to Läwen. Together we harvested many healing herbs for my people, like horehound for coughs and colds, rose hips for headaches and cramps, fennel for colds and heart ailments, and valerian as a tranquilizer or sleep medicine. I was also a midwife of both life and death. I helped my sisters give birth and eased our people into death. What a privilege it was!"

"What a beautiful story! Thank you for sharing it with me. It seems like you were well respected and honored in your clan. Yet now you seem so sad."

A darkness and agony appear in Grünthrad's eyes, and she begins to weep. "Everything changed. It is too painful to talk about right now. I must leave."

Abruptly she departs, sobbing.

7

Christianization
of the Saxons

It is easy and delightful to imagine all the surprising traits and experiences that I share with my Saxon ancestors. It makes me feel connected and special. But, with the connections also come the hard realities, the times of struggle, pain, and death that they endured. My research soon revealed those sobering realities.

I will forever be grateful to Rita Nakashima Brock and Rebecca Ann Parker, the authors of the book *Saving Paradise: How Christianity Traded Love of This World for Crucifixion and Empire*. When I read it over ten years ago, I found the first indication of the Saxons' ultimate struggle against their Christian conquerors. This struggle was the one that led to their annihilation as a people. And it came at the hand of the Catholic Church, the very institution that has been a big part of my life. This connection was difficult for me to absorb. But it was crucial to my healing journey that I do so. Perhaps it may be to yours as well.

The Marriage of Christianity and Power

Here is what I have come to understand.

The Romans first brought Christianity to the Celtic and Germanic peoples of northern Europe before the fall of the Roman Empire in the fifth century. But this Christianity was not exactly the Christianity that Jesus preached, a message of love, compassion, justice, nonviolence, and inclusivity. As the centuries proceeded, this original Christianity acquired more rules and laws, designed to standardize the religion. Then when Constantine became the Roman emperor in the fourth century, he converted to Christianity and declared Christianity a legitimate religion of the empire. It was thought at the time that this was a major win for the Christians, who had endured so much suffering and persecution at the hands of the Romans through the centuries. Now, they believed, they could practice their religion freely.

In 380, the emperor Theodosius went further and declared Christianity the official religion of the empire and banned paganism. This sounds like another win for the Christians. But, with this move, church and state had entered into a partnership that did not always adhere to the principles of Jesus. Since the church and state had become almost synonymous, they reinforced each other rather than being a healthy challenge to each other, and tragically became a blueprint for future ages.

The church now had political status. And since it had begun to assert that no one could get to heaven except by being a member of the church, its hierarchy felt a duty to make sure that all peoples conquered by the empire would also embrace Christianity. Often missionaries would accompany the soldiers to convert the northern tribes of Europe from their pagan and, in their minds, godless ways. If these people resisted, as they often did, then the soldiers of the empire had the duty to force them to convert, by whatever means necessary.

Thus was born "Christian imperialism." Religious imperialism of any kind is a state of mind in which conquerors believe that their religion is the only correct one, and thus everyone should believe in and convert to their religion. When the defeated peoples resist, any method, no matter how harsh, may be used to correct their waywardness or sinfulness. The conquering force believes that God is on their side.

Christianity and the Saxons

The Saxons had been defeated in numerous battles with the Romans before the fifth century, and each time were made to become Christian. But they resisted giving up on their spirituality totally. Nakashima Brock and Parker put it this way: "During Roman times, the Saxons had embraced Christianity, but their Christianity was a hybrid based on oral tradition rather than written texts. Their religious practices mixed pagan nature religion, which centered on great holy trees and sacred springs, with Christian folk traditions adapted from their early contact with Christians." (225)

When Roman rule crumbled in the fifth century, Irish, Scottish, and English missionaries, who had been converted earlier by the Romans, continued to spread Christianity by trying to convert the northern tribes. It wasn't easy. The religion the Saxons already practiced was an Indigenous religion, which was very different from the Christian religion. Carole Cusack, an Australian historian of religion, explains this distinction in her article titled "Pagan Saxon Resistance to Charlemagne's Mission: 'Indigenous' Religion and 'World' Religion in the Early Middle Ages."

> "Indigenous" literally means to be born of a
> place, and the ideal-type indigenous religions

> are particular, tribal, and land-based. . . . They
> also may be this-worldly, orally transmitted,
> non-proselytizing, and . . . pluralist. . . In
> contrast, the ideal-type world religions [like
> Christianity] are characterized by written
> scriptures, systematic theology, proselyti-
> zation, other-worldliness, elite orientation,
> [and] exclusivism. (35–36)

Put simply, these two types of religion were poles apart. The Saxons didn't want an "other-worldly" religion. They loved life on this earth and saw no reason to abandon their gods and goddesses and their natural way of life.

By the eighth century, efforts to convert the Saxons became more desperate and extreme. In 719, Boniface, an English monk, traveled to Saxony to bring a "correct" Christianity to the people. Eventually, to disabuse the Saxons of their pagan practices, he cut down one of their sacred oak trees, the mighty Oak of Thunor, in the southwest part of Saxon territory. The Saxons were horrified! This sacrilege only deepened their anger and resistance.

Interestingly, my hometown parish is named Saint Boniface. Every year we as a parish celebrated Saint Boniface as a great saint. I wonder what effect that name would have had on us descendants of the Saxons if we had understood what Boniface actually did to our traditional spirituality.

Enter the Franks

To the south of the Saxons, in what is now France, lay the land of the Franks. The Franks had been expanding their territory and building their power across Europe for centuries, oftentimes skirmishing with the Saxons in this endeavor. Under

Charles Martel and his son Pippin III of the Carolingian dynasty, the Franks ramped up their efforts and sought to establish a new empire in Europe. The Saxons stood in the way of this goal and needed to be subdued. But the Saxons were a fiercely independent people and were not about to cede their territory. The result was the escalation of brutal tactics on both sides.

In 772, Pippin's son, Charles the Great, also called Charlemagne, took over the quest for empire. And, since his Carolingian Frankish family dynasty had converted to Christianity in earlier centuries, Charlemagne also escalated his efforts to convert the pagan peoples he conquered to his religion. The Frankish nobility and its armies began to combine their Christian faith with their military pursuits. As a result, missionaries were accompanied by armed soldiers who carried out forced "conversion" through military might. These were not the Crusades, but certainly laid the groundwork for what was to come.

According to some scholars, Charlemagne's vision was to either convert the Saxons from their wrong beliefs or eradicate them. In 772 Charlemagne and his troops attacked the Saxons at the site of their great shrine, called the Irminsul, near Paderborn. The Irminsul was a large pillar or oak tree trunk that most likely represented the cosmic tree or the tree of life, something that is found in many Indigenous religions. This particular tree was the heart of the Saxon religion. At this site, Charlemagne's soldiers defeated the Saxon warriors, struck down the oak, and destroyed the shrine. Then they rounded up all the Saxons hiding nearby and forced them to be baptized under threat of death. All of this was a terrible but real example of Christian imperialism.

Still, the Saxons were resilient and did not capitulate. They soon attacked the Franks, who then counterattacked, and then the Saxons attacked again. This pattern went on for thirty-three years. To make things worse, Charlemagne, seeing himself as the ruler of the Saxons, issued a law code that Nakashima Brock and Parker explain "forbade the Saxons from engaging in their traditional religious activities and burial practices. The prescribed punishments were extreme. To refuse baptism or to eat meat during Lent merited the death sentence." (229)

Saxon nobles were more easily converted to Christianity because they were promised administrative positions in the new empire. Freemen and peasants, on the other hand, were more faithful to their traditional religion and continued to resist. They were led in this effort by a man named Widukind of Westphalia. Widukind had a close alliance with the Danes, who were very powerful at this time. He became a folk hero for many centuries because of his bravery leading the Saxons against Charlemagne.

The Saxon nobles entered into many treaties with the Franks over the years, but the middle and lower classes broke most of these treaties, causing Charlemagne to become more and more angry and frustrated. In 782, he carried out a major counterattack on the Saxons. At Verden, on the banks of the Weser River, he defeated the Saxons and had forty-five hundred of them beheaded in one day.

According to Nakashima Brock and Parker, the *Royal Frankish Annals*, written by the conquerors, claim that these killings were not a slaughter but a divine mission: "The more the Saxons were stricken by fear, the more the Christians were comforted and praised the Almighty God." (229)

Christian Imperialism Prevails

And still the Saxons rebelled. They desperately clung to their way of life and their religion. Between 783 and 785, there was constant warfare. In 785, Widukind, the Saxon hero, was finally baptized and swore fealty to Charlemagne. Eventually, in theory, the Saxons were absorbed into Carolingian Christianity, although many still clung to remnants of their former religion for decades. There were reports of outbreaks of "pagan" worship as late as the twelfth century.

The result of this brutal campaign was the eventual destruction of the Saxon culture, religion, and language. We in the twenty-first century are no strangers to this type of brutality in the name of religion and colonization. As Carole Cusack points out, "To a modern observer, Charlemagne's techniques are only too familiar. The Indigenous peoples of many modern colonized countries were killed in combat, had people relocated to reservations and mission stations, families torn apart as couples were segregated and their children taken from them, and traditional learning denigrated and suppressed." (46)

In this way, Christian imperialism destroyed the Saxon culture, religion, and language—my heritage.

This is the point in my research where everything goes dark.

The next time Grünthrad appears, she seems agitated and angry. She paces back and forth in front of me, muttering.

Finally, she blurts out, "I was killed at Verden! With my partner and most of our people! Can you imagine it? What a bloodbath!" Her rants turn to angry tears. "I can see it in my mind and heart to this day! I haunt the fields of Verden every night. I can still see my dead kin and smell the carnage. It is awful!"

Feeling inadequate, I reply, "I am so sorry. I had no idea."

"I am so angry! I just can't let it go," Grünthrad wails. "All we wanted was to remain on our land and preserve our way of life. But the Franks felt threatened by us. They wanted to take everything from us. Even our religion! But our gods and goddesses meant everything to us. We couldn't just abandon them, so we kept up our resistance. We knew it was dangerous, but we believed it was our duty."

"I can understand your resistance. Charles was attacking your very heart and soul."

"Ja, he was!" Grünthrad exclaims. "On that terrible day, Charles came at us again. We showed up at the field in Verden, some of us women included, prepared to defend ourselves. I am so glad I left my precious daughter, Läwen, with my mother back at our home, at least a half day's journey from Verden." She sighs. "We were defeated again. The soldiers rounded us up and told us we had to be baptized into the Christian faith and pay homage to Charles as king right there. We didn't want a king or his religion. So we refused again. Charles was enraged! He told his soldiers to make us lie down next to each other and *to behead all of us. A great cry rose up! Even his soldiers looked uncertain. But then the killing began." Grünthrad begins to sob. It lasts for a long time. I just sit with her in solidarity.*

Finally, she continues, "It disturbs me so much to remember this, but it seems that it is all I can think about. I can't find peace! I remember looking into the eyes of my Frankish executioner. All I could see was hate. Then I felt terrible pain, and everything went dark. Now I roam the killing field of Verden, crying, 'Why? Why?' But I get no answers."

"It is all so horrible! I can't even imagine the depth of your pain." We sit in silence for a while, and then Grünthrad leaves.

8

The Aftermath

I can see why Grünthrad's spirit and others continue to roam the killing fields of Verden. I have heard that places of bloodshed and carnage are often home to traumatized spirits who cannot attain peace. Not only that, the Saxon survivors, including her own kin, were left with nothing. Imagine how Grünthrad's mother and little Läwen must have felt.

Without an approved culture, language, homeland, or religion, their lives were reduced to mere survival. Their suffering was deep, since they had lost their families and their tribal structure. And because they were a defeated people, they weren't allowed to mourn and grieve their former way of life. They just had to get on with it. And they kept quiet, while underneath, their anger and grief simmered.

In Thomas Hübl's book *Healing Collective Trauma: A Process of Integrating Our Intergenerational and Cultural Wounds*, published in 2020, Dr. Judith Herman, a psychiatrist and researcher focused on trauma, states the following:

The ordinary response to atrocities is to

banish them from consciousness. Certain vi-
olations of the social compact are too terrible
to utter aloud: This is the meaning of the word
unspeakable. . . . Atrocities, however, refuse
to be buried. Equally as powerful as the desire
to deny atrocities is the conviction that denial
does not work. Folk wisdom is filled with
ghosts who refuse to rest in their graves until
their stories are told. (59)

I think this is probably both figuratively and literally true.
I believe that none of us can really rest until terrible secrets are
brought to light.

The original trauma, the beheadings at Verden, was just
the beginning of the suffering for the Saxons who survived that
event. Charlemagne, his successors, and the Catholic Church,
united in an unholy alliance, did everything in their power to
keep the Saxons subjugated. It is said that Charlemagne exiled
ten thousand Saxon survivors to other parts of the Frankish
kingdom. That displacement reinforced the trauma. The Saxons
were treated as second-class citizens or worse. They were pres-
sured to change their "evil" ways. All of that also reinforced the
trauma. But worst of all, they lost their identity and their source
of meaning. They must have wondered who they were now and
how they could make some sense of their lives.

A Core Loss

Being deprived of their religion and spirituality was among the
Saxons' most significant losses. They who saw the Divine in
nature, in a beautiful sunrise, in a healing rain, in the crops
they grew, in everything, were now confined to buildings and
texts, with a God not of this world. A harsh "Mother Church"

had replaced their beloved "Mother Earth." Peter Brown, professor of history at Princeton, talks about this in his book *The Rise of Western Christendom*:

> [Carolingian preachers] fulminated against
> trees and fountains, and against forms of divi-
> nation that gained access to the future through
> the close observation of the vagaries of animal
> and vegetable life. They imposed rhythms of
> work and leisure that ignored the slow turning
> of the sun, the moon, and the planets through
> the heavens, and that reflected, instead, a
> purely human time, linked to the deaths of
> outstanding individuals. (124–125)

In this way, the bishops and priests often became tyrants to the people, ruling how they lived their lives. No one could argue back; if they tried, they were accused of being sinners and were punished. To further keep the defeated Saxons in line, Charlemagne established Catholic bishoprics or dioceses in places important to the Saxons before their defeat, places like Paderborn, Münster, Bremen, Verden, and Osnabrück. In these places, the very oak trees that were cut down to prevent the defeated Saxons from continuing their "sinful ways" were used to build Christian churches. The Saxons were ordered to forget about their ancestors, who had been their source of wisdom and strength, and substitute instead the foreign saints of the Catholic Church.

From Hope to Terror

What made the Saxons' suffering even worse was that their defeat and almost total annihilation had come under the sign of the cross. For early Christians, the cross had been a sign of the Resurrection, an affirmation that life overcomes death. Jesus was usually depicted on a cross surrounded by images of paradise—the sun and moon, trees, streams, animals and birds. These images showed the beautiful nature that the Saxons also held sacred. Paradise could be found on Earth.

But since then, Christian armies had come conquering and killing, marching under a banner bearing the cross. As a result, the Saxons had come to associate Christianity with bloody genocide. It was unbearable for them to accept the cross as a sign of the Divine.

Nakashima Brock and Parker describe it this way:

> The cross—once a sign of life—became for
> them a sign of terror. . . . Within a few gener-
> ations of their forced conversion, the Saxons
> hewed an image of the tortured and dead
> body of Christ hanging from the tree. Pressed
> by violence into Christian obedience, the
> Saxons produced art that bore the marks of
> their baptism in blood. In the Gero Cross,
> their once-sacred oak was carved into an
> elegiac effigy of brutalization. (232)

This Gero Cross mentioned above was carved by an un-known artist from an oak tree in northwest Germany in the tenth century. Today, it can be found in the cathedral in Cologne, Germany. It is the earliest surviving crucifix to de-pict a bloody and mutilated Jesus rather than the triumphant Jesus of the Resurrection. This is the kind of crucifix that is familiar to most of us. In succeeding centuries, this style of crucifix became the norm, and featured more and more blood and gore, so much so that young children often ran away from the fearful image.

No longer did paradise and the Resurrection hold primary places in Christianity. Moreover, Carolingian theology featured Jesus as a victim, dying because of our sins. He no longer offered love, mercy, and justice, but instead represented judgment against sinful humanity.

A Christianity Based on Power

I can identify with many aspects of this aftermath to the Saxon defeat by the Christian Franks. My coming of age in the Catholic milieu of a small Midwestern town in the 1950s and 1960s, while idyllic in many ways, contained some of the same destructive mores and preaching topics that Grünthrad's descendants experienced in the Middle Ages. The similarity is almost eerie.

For example, the pastors in our hometown had ultimate power, since the town was almost all Catholic. Most of the early pastors were German-born and were often quite authoritarian. The first American-born pastor to lead our church served for thirty-one years, the whole span of my parents' childhood and early adulthood, but unfortunately, he, too, was authoritarian. I remember Mom and Dad describing him as a real tyrant. What he said, went, in both the church arena and in the civic arena. If he didn't like a certain family in the parish, he relentlessly persecuted the children of that family in the Catholic school.

To be fair, not all Catholics had domineering pastors like we had. Some Catholics remember their pastors as kind, gentle, and loving. And some had wonderful assistant pastors. We, too, had a kinder pastor for just a few years. But, unfortunately, the next pastor in my hometown parish was also harsh and uncompassionate. He, too, stayed for a long time as the earlier one had—fourteen years, the span of my whole childhood. He was the guy I mentioned in an earlier chapter, the one who was always focused on teaching about sex.

Only later did we learn that he had acted in a sexually inappropriate manner with some of the eighth-grade girls. By that time, some of the parents had forbidden their daughters to have individual contact with him. He reacted angrily by throwing their report cards at them in the church on the last day of school. Imagine how it must have felt to go to him for the sacraments, especially confession, baring your soul to a religious figure whom you didn't respect and actually feared, and who had perhaps abused and traumatized you.

Another similarity of my upbringing to the Saxon experience was the constant emphasis on sin. My hometown pastor's sermons and classes were filled with warnings against sinning, which to his mind seemed to lurk everywhere. Never did he acknowledge the goodness of the people. Even innocent pleasures like community dances brought forth his ire. People talk about "Catholic guilt," but I think it is really "Catholic shame." We were taught to constantly be on alert for the sins we were committing. We were told we were bad and needed to document our sins in frequent confession. Ironically, even believing in our own goodness was seen as bad. It was considered pride, which was one of the capital sins. We were, in effect, stuck, and being stuck is what shame is all about. We could never be good enough.

Only now as I write this book am I beginning to fully realize the harm that this often-dysfunctional Christian milieu and preaching has done to me. Fear and anxiety about sinning really implanted themselves in my being. I wanted to be good, but I couldn't trust myself. Thank God we had many good sisters and assistant pastors who taught God's love and gave us an alternate view of Christianity.

A green thread of hope appeared during this time period. Our parish was assigned an assistant pastor who was such a welcome change. Rev. Al Ede was young and fun. For example, he used to host sleigh-riding parties on my family's farm for the teenagers. He also was educated in the "new theology" that had been emerging since the Second Vatican Council. (I talk about this theology more in chapter 11.) He taught us high school students that God was good, that we were loved throughout history, and that we were good. He didn't have the same need to emphasize sin. He gave us hope.

But it still has taken me a long time to reorient my thinking and believing, and to heal.

Separate from the Natural World

Another issue that connects me with my Saxon kin is the issue of how nature was, or was not, acknowledged to have a place within the spiritual realm. Growing up, I had no idea that nature and spirituality are intrinsically entwined. I found comfort, peace, and inspiration in nature, but I didn't connect it to spirituality. The church had done such a thorough job of separating spirituality from nature that nature was often viewed in very negative terms, as needing to be controlled, or just ignored in order to focus on "things that mattered."

I now think of all the trees that the farmers cut down in the 1960s to expand their arable land. Dad used to talk about the lush canopy of trees that had overhung long stretches of our rural road in his younger years. I often picture that beautiful scene, but I never saw it with my eyes because it no longer existed by the time I was born. By then, our land looked a lot like the Saxon lands after the missionaries began to cut down the trees.

Before that destruction of Saxon lands, the great oaks had sustained the people. When Christian missionaries arrived in the Saxon homelands, they had the difficult task of bringing a totally foreign religion to a people who were satisfied with their own spirituality the way it was. James C. Russell, a professor of historical theology, explains the situation this way in *The Germanization of Early Medieval Christianity: A Sociohistorical Approach to Religious Transformation*: "When representatives of an . . . otherworldly, future-oriented Christian society confronted members of a past-oriented, this-worldly Germanic society, offering salvation from which the Germanic peoples did not desire to be saved, fundamental problems were inevitable." (177)

Because the Saxons were so resistant, the missionaries decided at first that the only way to "convert" them was to convince them that Christianity matched their Saxon life and spirituality. The missionaries decided to accommodate Saxon experience, at least initially. For example, the missionaries often usurped the "pagan" holy places and built churches on the same sites. They co-opted pagan holy days celebrating their gods and nature, and replaced them with holy days honoring the Virgin Mary and the saints. They incorporated the Saxon belief in petitioning and making offerings to the gods for all their needs by encouraging the people to go to the churches to petition the Christian God for their needs.

Christianity Turns Militaristic

According to Russell, the second phase of the Christianization plan for the Saxons, since it was thought that they were now "converted," was to be focused on ethical modification. Russell quotes historian of the Middle Ages Rosamond McKitterick as saying, "It is above all the consciousness of sin that is to be inculcated, the acknowledgment of the comparatively miserable and short nature of human life and the possibility of greater meaning lent it by Christianity and faith." (203)

So this is where all the emphasis on sin and punishment began! This policy diverges greatly from the Christianity of Jesus. And it was about to get more complicated. As Russell goes on to say, not only did the church Christianize the Saxons and other Germanic peoples, but in the process, the Germanic tribes actually Germanized Christianity. He cites the following quote by British historian and philosopher Robert A. Markus.

> [A number of Christian leaders recog-
> nized] that the conversion of their peoples
> to Christianity had done something to the
> religion to which they were converted. . . .
> They were . . . aware [that] . . . it had become
> the religion of a warrior nobility whose values
> and culture it had necessarily to absorb in the
> process of Christianizing them. (202–203)

This warrior ethos then became the norm throughout the church.

It is so unfortunate that much of the Saxon spirituality was lost as Saxons became Christian, like the love of nature, the belief in paradise on Earth, respect for women's wisdom, honoring of the ancestors, and the people's spiritual authority itself. Instead, the emphasis in Christianity evolved into being very warrior-like, emphasizing Christ as the king leading his followers to war. When I was a kid, the church had many militaristic hymns, including "Onward, Christian Soldiers."

> Onward, Christian soldiers, marching as to war,
> With the cross of Jesus going on before.
> Christ, the royal Master, leads against the foe;
> Forward into battle see His banners go. . . .
> Like a mighty army moves the Church of God.

We sang songs like these with great enthusiasm, never recognizing the discrepancy between Jesus's own compassion and love of sinners and the beliefs we had come to embrace.

Power Takes the Reins

These examples in the development of Christianity after the Saxon defeat—shunning nature, corrupting paradise, choosing power over love, emphasizing sin, militarizing Jesus—all took the church down a dangerous road, and brought about further loss of our spiritual authority. The balance that is needed in any successful system or institution gave way to a very one-sided hierarchical structure. The natural strength and energy of the Saxons was either beaten down or diverted into militarism and aggression. The people were worn down and traumatized, and no doubt felt stuck. They learned to give in and to be silent. Eventually, they would have no longer remembered that their lives could be any different.

The novel *Confessions of a Pagan Nun* by Kate Horsley features a fictional soliloquy of a Germanic pagan nun. Even though the novel is set in a time when the missionaries had just begun the conversion of "pagans," it illustrates something of what the defeated Saxons must have also experienced from a hierarchical church determined to crush their beliefs and way of life.

> I have seen that the Christian philosophy of the bishops compels people to turn away from the earth toward heaven. It encourages a view of earth as a place of degradation and temptation. . . . And it seems curious to me that those who condemn this earth and its goods most vehemently and greedily amass those

goods. . . . The chieftains who used to know
the earth as their wife now use her as mis-
tress. I fear that the cleverest means of power
will be for the Christians to use their wealth
to own the weapons and war beasts that will
give them dominance over the distribution of
grain and land. (164–165)

Where does all this trauma go? The people coped by re-
pressing their feelings and going along with their enslavement
to the church and the empire. What message is in this for us?

When Grünthrad appears this time, she seems exhausted with grief. "Thank you for listening to me. I have had no one for such a long time."

"I am glad I could be of some help." Then moving gently into the more difficult story, I ask, "Grünthrad, what happened to your daughter, Läwen? You said she was safe, but what was it like for her after the massacre?"

Grünthrad sighs deeply. "She was so sad. I was there with her every day, though she couldn't see me nor sense my presence. She kept asking where her mother and father had gone. She had nightmares every night for a long time. My mother and the rest of the clan were so overwhelmed and grief-stricken that they could barely function." Tears appear in her eyes.

"It must have been heartbreaking for them."

"Ja, it was," she says, pausing for a while. Suddenly, her anger erupts again. "They weren't even allowed to grieve! Instead, they were made to confess their 'sins.' What sins? They were good people! They couldn't go to their gods for comfort. They were forced to go into what the Franks called a church and just sit there quietly, while the priest preached at them and told them how bad they were. They couldn't say a thing. It was awful!"

Grünthrad pauses, looking dejected. But after a while, she sits taller, and when she speaks again, her voice sounds more composed. "My kinfolk were angry, and they rebelled in secret ways. My mother and the other women clan members taught the young girls the old ways. Läwen, too, became a healer, though always in secret. But I could see the spark in her eyes.

I believe she inherited our clan's strength, independence, and courage. She had to go along with the rule-bound religion, but in her heart, she knew that what she was being taught by the conquerors was not right. Inwardly she raged, while outwardly she managed a smile."

"That must have been so difficult."

When she continues, her tone is a little lighter, and there is the beginning of a smile on her face. "But Läwen kept sneaking out to her favorite trees—those that were left after the destruction. She prayed to our gods in her heart. And she and the other young people would often create a secret language among themselves, one only they understood. That way they could cling to some power over the Franks. And some hope."

"I have read that other defeated people have done the same thing. The creation of a language is a form of resistance, like the resistance you practiced all along."

Grünthrad smiles. "Ja, I am very proud of her." She paused. "But the hope didn't last."

9

Intergenerational Trauma

My encounters with Grünthrad made me wonder, *Where does all this trauma go? What can I learn from what modern researchers are saying about the effects of trauma on the traumatized person's descendants?*

There has been much research done in the last four or five decades about intergenerational trauma. Medicine, physiology, psychology, spirituality, social work, and other academic disciplines have tried to answer the questions of how a catastrophic event in the past influences survivors and their descendants to the present day.

A notable resource on this topic is Thomas Hübl's aforementioned book, *Healing Collective Trauma*. In it, Hübl—a modern mystic, spiritual teacher, training facilitator, and expert on trauma, who integrates wisdom traditions with science—says that trauma affects the survival or animal part of the brain. After a traumatic event, our ability to decode danger signals is disturbed. "[T]rauma has the power to change the central nervous system. It alters the way we assimilate memory and leaves us highly reactive to any stimuli that mirrors, however unconsciously, the original experience." (15)

This means that if we don't feel safe and don't detect a supportive social system, we unconsciously fall into the fight-or-flight response, a response from the sympathetic nervous system that is meant to protect us. When the danger situation goes on for a long time, we keep repeating these behaviors in order to survive. Eventually, these behaviors get imprinted in the body. Even when things are good, the person is still in fight-or-flight mode. These behaviors then get passed down to their children and other descendants through DNA, community expectations, rigid social systems, and the stories they tell themselves about the world and about who they are in it.

This process is called intergenerational trauma. It ensues when survivors of the original trauma don't have the freedom, opportunities, resources, or resilience to heal their trauma. Intergenerational trauma is often buried in silence or explodes in rage. Its many effects may include broken relationships, family secrets, substance abuse, violence, and physical ailments. The descendants of the individuals who were traumatized often don't know where their own fear, anxiety, and problematic behaviors originated. Have you ever experienced this? I certainly have. And my desire for healing has caused me to want to learn more—including where these feelings and behaviors began.

Trauma's Effects Over the Generations

When intergenerational trauma is experienced by whole groups of people over time and across generations, as it was for Grünthrad and her fellow Saxons, it is also called historical trauma. Historical trauma is the result of forces that include war, imperialism, colonization, subjugation, occupation, and enslavement. You and I can probably think of many examples of historical trauma, both in the past and still very real in the present. There are many people and groups who have experienced not one or two traumatic events, but a lifetime and more of trauma and abuse.

In the US, we need look no further than our African American and Native American sisters and brothers. Hübl states the following:

> When the people of a particular culture or tradition have been torn from their homes and lands, when their . . . burial places, religious centers, or sacred sites have been desecrated or denied them, when their language, rituals, customs have been banned, forbidden, or forgotten, when they and their people have been separated, humiliated, brutalized, tortured, or murdered, a traumatic wound cleaves the collective psyche—scarring both persecuted and persecutor—and will be carried and transmitted for many generations. (67–68)

In such cases, the suffering of one generation is passed down to their children and to their children's children.

Historical trauma is a major scar on all our psyches, whether it is acknowledged or not, whether a person is a victim or a perpetrator. We have all inherited the trauma. Later in this book, I will address what can be done about it. But for now, let us go back to the defeated Saxons.

Silence, Denial, and Forgetting

To survive, the Saxons learned to keep silent, to not talk about the massacre and the trauma. They didn't want to dwell on the pain, and it was often dangerous to speak against the victors. So they kept the secrets of their suffering from their families, likely claiming some version of "It's not so bad" (perhaps while sobbing when alone at night).

Saxon descendants of such survivors of trauma inherited this pattern of silence, denial, and forgetting. These tactics were used by the remaining Saxons to survive violence and oppression, but they also became the normal behavior of their people, which led their descendants to use the same unhelpful tactics to deal with their own challenges—don't discuss, don't feel, keep secrets, cut off relationships. Elaine Enns and Ched Myers, writers, activists, and facilitators in restorative justice and social change, state this in their book *Healing Haunted Histories: A Settler Discipleship of Decolonization*, saying, "Hauntings inhabit silences as well as testimonies." (66)

Reading Hübl's book and others helped me to understand that I probably have indeed inherited some of the trauma my ancestors originally experienced.

For example, remember the scene when I learned from my mother that she preferred to take care of the cooking and other household tasks on her own, and that I should "go out and play"? Because of her experience in her family, Mom took the total burden of work on herself, while I was taught to basically not work too hard. In school I worked hard and achieved, but in domestic situations, I felt useless. Might this echo the same learned helplessness that the Saxons had to adopt in order to survive—just go along and do what you're told?

Wrestling with Joy

An experience I had in 2005 taught me some valuable insights about myself and my own ways of denying myself and my experiences. A religious sister friend and I went to Los

Angeles for a therapy conference. We also scheduled in two extra days for play. One day she chose Disneyland, and the next day I chose *The Price Is Right*. I love games and game shows, so it was a natural choice. Getting to the show was a process filled with huge challenges. We had to get up at 2:30 a.m. in order to be the first people in line. The line was outside on the street, and it was cold—forty degrees. (I thought LA was warm!) The nearest bathroom was at a bakery across the street that didn't open till 4:30 a.m. We finally filed into the studio nine hours later. I was chosen as a contestant, and I won some prizes—a bedroom suite and a sapphire-and-diamond ring.

I was totally excited and happy to be on the show and to win—a normal reaction. I learned that I can be very confident, capable, and charming when I'm passionate about something. But it was my later reaction that caught me off guard. When we got back to the hotel, I plunged down from the high and went into an anxiety meltdown. *What have I done?* I thought. *What am I going to do with these luxurious gifts? How am I going to pay the luxury tax? How will I tell the community that they have to pay that tax for me?* We share all our money, and I was overwhelmed with worry about what now seemed like a burden on the group that I had incurred because I'd wanted to do something for myself.

The questions went on. And they went deeper. *Have I shown off? Have I been too proud? Am I being selfish? Have I enjoyed the experience too much? What will the community think about me?* Later, I realized that in the midst of happiness, I had fallen back into the more-familiar victim stance I had once been taught, and which had been reinforced in me by religious messaging. Joy had very quickly transformed into guilt and shame, as it has for me on many occasions. This progression leads to anxiety even when the danger I perceive is minimal. My mind and body ramp up. *What should I do next?*

Will I be okay? Am I overstepping my boundaries? Am I trying to be more than I am?

These kinds of responses have been programmed into my body and mind, through messages and expectations received from church, society, and family, and reinforced through stories I tell myself. *I'm alone. I don't have what I need. I can't figure it out. I will do it wrong.*

In the years since that day in LA, however, I've learned to tell myself different stories, to change the narrative. Now, I say to myself things like *I am capable. I am not alone. I am a good person. I am loved. It's okay to be angry and express it.* (I'm still new to this last one.) I practice deep breathing, take meditative walks, and loosen my jaw by peeling my tongue off the roof of my mouth. (Did you know that was a thing?) I also focus on the goodness of people around me and the goodness in the world. I have learned how to regulate my reactions and extreme responses so that I can live life more freely and joyfully.

Your Trauma and Mine

As I've said before, I have not experienced any major trauma, so I believe that many of my trauma responses may have been passed down my family tree. What about you? Can you pinpoint trauma in your own family tree that may still influence or even control you to this day? How have you seen it manifest itself?

Perhaps it shows up in addictions, anxiety, depression, broken family relationships, violence, destructive family secrets, or physical illnesses. Or you may feel stuck. According to James A. Houck Jr., "This [stuck] feeling of being trapped in linear time can extend to days, months, years, decades and even centuries, as past, present and future generations often bear the scars of *once upon a time*." (xi)

"Once upon a time," Läwen and her Saxon community experienced terrible trauma, and because they were a defeated people, they were not able to process their loss and heal from it. They just had to go on. To do that, they needed to forget, to banish the trauma from their consciousness. Nevertheless, the trauma was still there and was passed down to their children and their children's children, all the way down to me. Could this also apply to your ancestors, and all the way down to you?

Are we Western white Christian women (and men) willing to get beyond our denial? Are we willing to recognize and heal the traumas that we have personally endured or inherited from our ancestors? This is necessary work if we want to bring about a better world.

When Grünthrad appears again, I ask, "Earlier you mentioned that 'the hope didn't last.' What did you mean by that?"

"I meant that the hope and motivation to resist didn't last into the future generations. My daughter Läwen's own children and grandchildren began to pull away from the old beliefs and practices. They learned to be submissive to Christian authorities. This was very difficult for me to witness. I was outraged, and at the same time very sad."

She continues on, "Läwen was sad, too, but what could she do? When she tried to teach her grandchildren what she knew to be true, they got scared and felt ashamed. After all, hadn't the priests told them that the old ways were evil? They didn't want to sin, and they tried to convince Läwen not to sin either. Can you believe it? They weren't even allowed to remember me. That hurt deeply, and I still feel the pain to this day."

"I am so sorry! It must be terrible for you."

Now Grünthrad seems more resigned. "I suppose their reaction was not unfounded. It had become dangerous to embrace any of the old ways. Women were attacked by crowds for gathering herbs for medicines." Just like that, Grünthrad's anger is back. "What's wrong with receiving gifts from Mother Earth? I don't understand!" she shouts.

"I can see why you are outraged," I say. "All that you knew and considered holy was now considered evil. Plus as time went on, your descendants began to forget about the horror you suffered. At the same time, they seemed to have embodied a shame hidden deep within. They began to see themselves as bad, but they weren't sure why."

"*Ja!*" *she replies.* "*I rarely saw them smile anymore. They were more and more sad and angry. And they couldn't talk about the trauma. Therefore, it got stuck in their hearts.*" *She sighs deeply.* "*Before Verden, my people would smile a lot and have so much fun together. I miss that.*"

"*I'm glad you are telling me your story, both the bad and the good,*" *I muse.* "*I am recognizing that some of your pain and trauma has continued on through the generations. Something that horrible that hasn't been healed has to go somewhere. I believed so long that something was wrong with me, though there was no evidence of anything. That is probably the unhealed shame passed down through the centuries. I guess we are more connected than I thought.*"

Part Two

10

Resilience

We have all been traumatized at some level at various times, but what can we do to address that trauma? How do we hang on to life and hope in the midst of trauma?

In the case of the Saxon survivors, they hung on by a thread—what I have described as a green thread. Imagine a "green thread" as the filament of hope that runs through life, just like the green thread Grünthrad's mother sewed into her tunic. In Christian terms, this thread is called the Spirit of God, or the Holy Spirit, or God's grace. This is the divine force that brings life to us. No matter how bad circumstances get, in the midst can be found a green thread—maybe even more than one. This thread may not be easy to find, but it is there, waiting for you.

In the present-day study of "intergenerational trauma," the other side of trauma is called "resilience." Resilience is defined as the power within people and systems that helps us adapt to challenges that threaten our functioning and our very survival. It is the capacity to survive and even thrive in the midst of darkness and difficulty. It is the life force within us, God's life force. This resilience is the green thread in all of our lives. As Hübl states, "The twin legacy of trauma and resilience bears out in every human's ancestral DNA and in every culture's psychic inheritance." (14)

Resilience empowers us to face trauma, tell our painful stories, remember our uplifting stories, perform healing rituals together, and recognize that we are one and can help each other. Part of the process is "re-membering," which, as touched on earlier, is a term some feminist scholars use to mean recovering and bringing back into the story the memory of women and other discounted peoples who have been forgotten. Remembering involves listening to these people's stories, as well as recognizing and reclaiming their goodness, strength, and power that has always been within us, but which we forgot because of the trauma and its effects on us, seen and unseen. I call that resilience "the green thread."

The thread is always there. However, we sometimes need to be challenged to wake up from our lethargy or forgetfulness about who we really are in order to embrace courage and resilience. Let me give two illustrations of what I mean.

Examples of Resilience

I described in earlier chapters how I was burdened with shame most of my life. But that was not always the case. I remember that one day—in the midst of my shame narrative, as I was telling myself how bad and lacking I was—I also got in touch with my true self, my creative and energetic self. It was a simple act of resilience.

Here's what happened. When I was sixteen, I tried out for cheerleading. I loved attending basketball games and watching the game and the cheerleaders. It was so exciting! I wanted to be involved. I knew I had natural rhythm. And, to be honest, it was a very small school, and the odds of making the squad were fairly good. So I tried out, and, to my delight, I made the team.

Looking back now, I realize what an audacious move that was for me. I, who often hid in shame, was putting myself in front of a crowd and essentially saying, "Look at me." This is shame's worst nightmare, because shame's signature is hiding, trying not to be seen. But I was so passionate about the mission of working with a group of girls to cheer on our team that for once I didn't let shame interfere. Somehow, I let my resilience and courage emerge. Grünthrad would have been proud!

Another personal example is the story I told about my experience on *The Price Is Right*. Though I initially let my feelings of anxiety and shame overwhelm my joy and steal the delight of that passionate experience, I later managed to work through it by re-membering the truth of what had actually happened almost twenty years before. In the intervening years, I've actually learned to embrace the joy and confidence I felt that day, instead of the shame. I remember the courage and enthusiasm it took to try out for the show in the first place. This experience has now become a resilience narrative for me, one I can remember and tell others.

As I was writing this, I realized that I had used the word "passionate" in referring to both of my examples of resilience. This informs me that maybe these words, "resilience" and "passionate," go together in some way. I'm not a parent, but I imagine that even if you are feeling down or deflated, if your child needs you, you'll do whatever it takes to help them. You'll exhibit great energy, courage, and confidence, if only for that moment.

This resilience is programmed into us. We just have to choose it. Author Robert Ellsberg cites Howard Thurman, twentieth-century theologian, mystic, and civil rights activist, as having challenged us with the words, "Don't ask what the world needs. Ask what makes you come alive, and go do it. Because what the world needs is people who have come alive." (*Give Us This Day*, April 10, 2021)

Claiming Your Passion

Does this feel like a foreign concept: doing what you're passionate about rather than just following the expectations of others? That would be totally understandable because women, especially, have been schooled to look to others for definition, be that in the role of good mother, good wife, good religious sister, follower, handmaid, etc. And Christianity has often reinforced that message.

For example, the church lists pride as one of the capital sins. Of course, it is not good for anyone to be egotistical and self-absorbed. But Christian feminist writers have pointed to the fact that pride may be more likely a sin of the male elite, while for women and other disenfranchised groups, the worse sin would be not claiming our God-given goodness and authority. That concept has stuck with me for a long time and rings true in my life.

For women, claiming our resilience means acknowledging actual reality and then getting beyond the silences and the false narratives in order to get to the heart of things, wherein lie God and our true self, and our spiritual authority. Now that I'm thinking about all this, I believe I was given the answer of how to do this way back in 1988, at the school board retreat in Oklahoma City. Or rather, I was given the question.

The question I was asked was this: "What are you passionate about?" It is what we are passionate about that points to resilience, because that's what we have energy for, that is what we'll risk our settled lives for, that is what leads us to our true call in life.

Bodies of Resistance

Resilience is not just a personal opportunity. Whole groups of people through the centuries have found resilience in the midst of oppression and trauma. Winona La Duke, an economist, environmentalist, writer, and member of the Ojibwe White Earth people of Minnesota, works for justice for Indigenous peoples. In 2021, I attended a conference at which La Duke spoke. While I don't have a recording of that event, I recall that, while reflecting on Native American experience, she said something to the effect of "They pushed us into the ground, but they forgot we were seeds." (White Privilege Conference, La Crosse, WI, 2021) What better way to speak of resilience?

The Saxons, too, continued to resist the power that had subdued them and supposedly wiped out their culture. I've already noted that they continued to carry out armed resistance in the first centuries after their defeat. But the Saxons also proclaimed their resistance through symbols that had hidden meaning that only they understood fully.

Remember the Gero Cross from chapter 8, carved in the tenth century, the first known cross to depict a bloody and suffering Jesus? On the outside, the cross depicted submission. But according to Nakashima Brock and Parker, "As a hidden symbol of resistance, the image preserved the Saxons' experience at the hands of their oppressors. It unveiled Christ as a co-sufferer with them in their struggles with the colonizing empire." (252–253) They knew, too, that in the end, Christ had risen. They believed that the conquering power would not triumph.

This is very similar to the resilience shown by African slaves in the US. Amid unspeakable torture, lack of freedom, and denigration of their very being, these slaves gathered together in the churches and began to pray and sing a similar theme of resistance. Their sermons emphasized the Exodus story—speaking about how God had led them through the desert and offering hope that they would eventually see the Promised Land. Their spirituals sang of Jesus who suffered with them and overcame death. This awareness gave them the strength, resilience, courage, and hope to go on living.

The Resilience of Hidden Resistance

The Saxons were able to carry out hidden resistance through poetry and stories, which are able to carry multiple meanings and can encompass both compliance and protest in the same work. One of the only Saxon literary works that has survived, called the *Heliand* (meaning the "healer" or the "savior"), appeared to depict compliance but, to those in the know, exhibited resistance. Nakashima Brock and Parker describe the *Heliand* this way:

> [The *Heliand* is] a mid-ninth-century epic in rhythmic verse marked for singing. . . . [Written in a Germanic dialect] . . . the *Heliand* retells a [Syrian text] that synthesized the four Gospels into one story. . . . To write in German instead of Latin, the official language of Carolingian Christianity, was itself an act of defiance. In addition, . . . this poem reaches into the past to depict an ethics of loyalty and camaraderie once practiced in traditional Saxon culture. (240–241)

The *Heliand* celebrated a Gospel in which paradise lived in this world. This wasn't the Gospel being preached by the Carolingians, so holding onto this loving Gospel, too, was a form of resilience.

Passion and Resilience

Even in the darkest of times, the green thread of life continues to weave hope through our own lives and in and among the people. For example, even when I was engulfed in my shame narrative, I knew I loved school and was good at learning. I was able to really excel and become a leader in that arena. There I felt alive and confident. Also, I loved sports, an interest I inherited from my dad, and I participated whenever I could. Even when I wasn't very good at a certain sport, I often tried anyway. For example, I had been pretty good at softball in grade school. But as I got older, more girls got better than I, but I still participated. Instead of feeling ashamed of what I couldn't do, I celebrated what I could do, and the reward was getting to be part of a team.

Here's another example. In high school, I knew I wasn't a good actress, but I wanted to be in the school play, *Pride and Prejudice*, because many of my friends were. I wanted to hang out with them backstage. So, instead of trying out for one of the more prominent parts, I tried out for the maid's role. The drama teacher was surprised but gave me the part. (Of course, no one else wanted it.) I really did well on my three lines—"You rang, sir." "Here is your tea, madam." "Right away, sir." And I had a great time backstage with my friends. Win-win!

You can see that, even as I was very aware of my shame in larger social situations and in the spiritual arena, I relied on my passion for learning and for sports and cheerleading and other peer activities. These areas of my life served as a green thread for me and helped remind me of my resilience within. I also relied on my family and friends and their support. However, to become an integrated human being and a whole person, I needed to embrace the long and difficult journey of healing that part of me that kept putting me down. This led me to the process of imagining myself connected with my ancestor Grünthrad, which I have been sharing, and will continue to share, with you.

Traveling Through History with Grünthrad

In this second part of the book, I journey with Grünthrad through the history of her descendants and my ancestors, focusing mostly on the experience of women, since women's experiences are what I know personally. Because women were often left out of historical narratives, I try to find their true stories, what kept them bound, and what set them free—the green thread of the Spirit constantly bringing about new life. And since what has kept me and so many other women and men bound for centuries has been patriarchy and Christian imperialism, I also concentrate my journey on uncovering how these two systems served to deny our spiritual authority, and how women and men were able to nurture their spiritual authority in the midst of it. In addition, where I am able, I will highlight people from northwest Germany, most probably my Saxon ancestors.

Along the way, I adopt a stance revealed to me by Dorothee Sölle, a northwest German theologian and an activist in peace and ecological movements, in her excellent book *The Silent Cry: Mysticism and Resistance*. Dorothee learned the concept of "a hermeneutic of suspicion." "Hermeneutic" is a big word that simply refers to "the study and establishment of the principles by which a sacred book is to be interpreted." (Britannica. com) As Sölle states, "The hermeneutic of suspicion . . . suspect[s] every text, every tradition, in terms of its legitimizing role in promoting the domination of a particular tradition." (46) In other words, the hermeneutics of suspicion call us to ask: Who stands to benefit from this text as it is written?

The various Christian theologies, such as Christian feminist

theology, Black Womanist theology, and Latin American liberation theology, that were formed by those on the underside
of society (women, the poor, the marginalized, people of color)
have employed this suspicion regarding the official Christian
texts. For example, Christian feminist theology recognized
that very few women were included in the Bible, and when
they were, they were often not named personally—i.e., the
Samaritan woman, the woman with a hemorrhage, the mother
of James and John. And when they *were* named, as in the case
of Mary Magdalene, they were often shown in a bad light. As a
result, when women read the Scriptures now, they recognize,
unconsciously at least, that they are not considered as important as men.

Once women become aware of this, they read the Scriptures
thereafter with a "hermeneutic of suspicion," always interpret-
ing the text for themselves and other women in order to feel
included. Later, after they feel they belong, women can then
employ what Sölle calls a "hermeneutic of hunger." According
to Sölle, "Suspicion is appropriate wherever religion exercises
unrestricted, total control over the life of women. [But then]
our inquiry needs a different point of departure. . . . I try to
depict a hermeneutic of hunger. . . . The hermeneutics of the
poor is one of hunger for bread and liberation." (48)

This idea of a hermeneutic of hunger speaks to me at a
deep level. Once I had learned to exercise the hermeneutic of
suspicion about Christian texts, I was able to interpret them to
include my experience. I could ask myself, "What is the wisdom of this text, and how does it apply to me in the twenty-
first century?" But that method only goes so far. After asking
questions of the text, I needed to ask questions of myself.

Now I needed to ask myself (as Jesus asks in the Scriptures),
*What is it I desire? For what does my soul, my deepest self,
hunger? What deep need will drive me forward to act?* It is important to ask these questions in order to reclaim ourselves

and our spiritual authority. As Sölle continues, "It is not suspicion that turns people away from the church; it is hunger that drives them to seek help wherever their dignity and their right to have a life are being respected." (48)

The answer to the question "What is it you desire?" requires deep exploration within. It asks us to become "seekers." But the answer to the question is not always readily accessible. It is not something superficial, like money, fame, or even happiness. At my yearly retreat, which is required for women religious, the retreat director often asks me this same question, and I usually find it hard to answer easily or immediately. Answering this takes quiet, prayer, and looking deeply within to find God's desire for me. It is such a blessing to receive a sense of God's desire for me and to understand that God is already waiting to grant that desire.

So, as I walk with Grünthrad through the centuries of trauma and resilience, I will be using both a hermeneutic of suspicion (finding out where we were traumatized) and a hermeneutic of hunger (discovering what has been luring us into life). I will highlight the actions of the hierarchical patriarchal church and its allies, powerful political white men of the time, which veered away from the church of Jesus and caused deep personal and spiritual suffering for the common people. I will also highlight how, at the same time, seemingly ordinary people were grasping the green thread of grace, hungering for the loving, compassionate, and merciful God, and using their inner knowing, their spiritual authority, to proclaim another way forward.

I've been thinking about Grünthrad a lot lately. Our time together has become very precious to me.

Grünthrad appears to be in a good mood when she arrives. She is walking more upright and is eager to begin our discussion. "It was good for me to learn about resilience," she says. "The way my descendants were able to embrace their strength enough to engage in resistance even though it was very difficult was inspiring to me. I am proud of them. This was probably their green thread at work."

"I believe it was," I reply. "And you are a green thread for me. Thank you."

I continue, "The first part of my book began to give me a glimpse of what you and my other ancestors endured. I am grateful that you broke your silence to help me understand. Much of this is new information for me, and it takes a while to sink in and become real for me. I ask myself, 'How does all this affect me? What is my trauma to uncover?' I guess the next part of this journey will lead me to my own resilience."

"We probably just need to keep walking, gradually getting to know my descendants and your ancestors," Grünthrad muses. "Our story of trauma and hopefully resilience will help us both."

"I am eager to continue the journey with you," I reply.

11

The Crusades and the Mystics

The centuries after Charlemagne killed the forty-five hundred Saxons at Verden and effectively began the destruction of their culture were very difficult times for the surviving Saxons.

Carolingian preachers continued to make sure that all the surviving Saxons were baptized into Christianity, under punishment of death. But this Christianity was not the Christianity of Jesus and his disciples. As we've seen, this version of Christianity emphasized sin and punishment rather than love and compassion. The surviving Saxons were taught that they were basically sinners, that they had to confess their many sins to the priests so they wouldn't go to hell. This is basically the same message I was taught almost a millennium later. I can't believe in that version of Christianity anymore; it is too toxic. I want to get back to the true Gospel message of love, mercy, and peace.

Disempowering the People

In order to consolidate its power and unify all parts of the empire, the church required the use of Latin as the language of the Mass. Since only learned clerics knew Latin and most people at the time were illiterate, the ordinary person needed to depend on the clerics for guidance and understanding in all things spiritual. This dependence was demonstrated at the Mass with the priest standing at the altar between God and the people with his back to them in order to be the "official" translator of God's message. This forced servility and blind obedience caused irreparable harm to the people's belief in their own direct relationship with God and therefore in their spiritual authority.

This Latin liturgy continued as the only language of the Catholic Church for more than a thousand years. I remember going to Mass in the 1950s and 1960s and using a missal with Latin on one side and the English translation on the other side. This format was designed to help us understand what was happening, and what was being said, in a ritual that was spoken in (what was to us) a foreign language. At least our generation had some help in comprehending the liturgy. But reading a translation was definitely not conducive to worshipping God.

In addition to the Latin liturgy, another way Catholics were kept in the dark was through the dearth of religious education in adulthood. Presumably the thinking was this: Why would the people need it? Catholics were to be dependent on clerics to tell them what to do.

Finally, in the 1960s, the Second Vatican Council recognized the importance of the laity in the church—that is, those who were not clergy—by referring to the whole church as the "people of God." In order for them to be fully involved and take their rightful leadership role in the church, however, lay Catholics needed to understand their religion. By the 1970s, parishes and Catholic high schools began to offer Catholic adult education classes.

My dad and mom attended these classes at our local Catholic high school in the late 1960s and 1970s. Their eyes were opened, and they loved these teachings, known as "new theology," which emphasized the love of God rather than God's judgment. It made so much more sense to them. But they deeply grieved all the time they had spent believing what wasn't true.

The Merging of Church and State

Those in the Middle Ages did not have the benefit of this more loving theology. Far from it. The entanglement between church and state, or Christian imperialism, continued to deepen. On Christmas Day 800, Pope Leo III named Charlemagne the emperor of the Holy Roman Empire, which was not Roman at all, but was rather an official joining of the church with the Carolingian empire. Eventually, because of constant infighting in this religious empire, the western part of the empire split from the eastern part, further fracturing Christianity.

In the western part of the empire, Charlemagne's immediate successors proved to be very ineffective rulers. With no major military power in the West, local rulers took over the governing of their small territories, and civil chaos ensued. Europe became a very dangerous place, and people felt powerless. Harry Rosenberg, former professor of history at Colorado State University, observes, "The end of the world seemed at hand. It was seriously expected by many as the year 1000 approached." (198) Unfortunately, the church could provide no spiritual resources or hope for the people.

A Familiar Bleakness

Does this situation in any way remind you of today's world? I remember when we were approaching our own turn of the millennium. No one knew what would happen as the calendar pages went from December 31, 1999, to January 1, 2000. Many of us were afraid that the internet would crash, an event that would affect all our vital services, including water, electricity, heat, food, communication, data storage, and security systems. People coped in different ways, including through feeling fear, ignoring the situation, or blaming someone. Others placed their trust in God.

Our situation today further reflects the chaos and loss that our ancestors endured, and we, too, lack the spiritual resources to help us cope. Every day we turn on the news to be confronted with yet another mass shooting or another unprovoked attack on people of color or of another religion. We are experiencing climate change in the form of massive droughts, heat waves, superstorms, rising oceans, land masses falling into the seas, crop failures, and more. Governments in the US and around the world are engaging in so much infighting that they don't have the will to collaborate in order to help their citizens.

How do we respond? Do we cower alone in fear? Do we rage outwardly and violently attack (in words or actions) those who don't agree with us or look like us or believe like us? Or do we trust in God and the goodwill of all those around us? Do we take Jesus's commands to heart—to love one another, to act justly, to work together for peace and equity for all? Do we claim our spiritual authority? This is the crucial decision we have to make every day.

Looking for Protection

In the Middle Ages, in order to protect themselves from Viking marauders from the north and from their own neighboring rulers, many kings and nobles believed they needed a standing military. Since the pope and the Catholic Church also owned extensive lands, they, too, felt the need for military protection.

Because of strained relations between the Carolingians and the Italian nobles, the church looked to the north for this protection. In this way, the papacy came to develop a close relationship with the Germanic rulers.

Because the former Saxons had gained a reputation as fierce fighters from all their years fighting the Franks, they were the ones tapped to be the papal protectors. I imagine that this must have seemed very strange to them. Consider with me the situation in which the former Saxon men found themselves. They were asked to defend the very group that had robbed them of their culture, language, and religion. Before, their people had been murdered for resisting; now, the men were praised by the people and rewarded by the nobles for their acts of violence.

Stories about this Saxon generation passed down to future generations lifted up the courage, daring, and heroic (often bloody) feats of these warriors. Yet I believe that underneath these acts was probably a seething, unacknowledged rage from the earlier trauma they had experienced. They had been told to forget, and perhaps on the surface they had. But, as is often the case when there's unresolved trauma, their actions were at odds with who they really were as persons.

And what about the former Saxon women? They, too, must have carried within them rage and loathing for their former conquerors. But they had to be quiet and go along with what was expected. They couldn't claim their own power and spiritual authority; the risk seemed too great.

A noble, strong, and talented people had been reduced to pawns, the men consumed with fighting and the women made to keep quiet. They were living as caricatures of themselves. These dynamics continued to contribute to a church that was becoming more and more unbalanced. The excessive focus on violence and anger in Europe and in the church often led to more violence.

A Holy War Begins

In the year 1095, the Eastern Christian emperor called on Pope Urban II for help in defeating the Turkish Muslims and transferring the ruling power in the Holy Land and Jerusalem back to the Christians. Pope Urban II acquiesced and called for a crusade, essentially a holy war. Kings, nobles, knights, clerics, and ordinary men who had been fighting each other were asked to defeat what was seen as a common threat to Christianity.

To help recruit enough fighting men, Pope Urban II and subsequent popes created both civil and religious incentives. As found in *Introduction to the History of Christianity*, edited by historian Tim Dowley, according to Robert G. Clouse, former professor of history at Indiana State University, these incentives included "immunity from taxes and debt payment, protection of crusaders' property and families, and especially the indulgence, which guaranteed the crusader's entry into heaven and reduced or abolished his time in purgatory." (228) In this way, as Nakashima Brock and Parker note, "War ceased being a sin and became a way to atone for sin. Killing became a mode of penance, a pathway to paradise." (264)

Over a period of two hundred years, a series of Crusades took place, sanctioned by the church. Some crusades resulted in victories, but most were unsuccessful, leaving much of the Holy Land under Muslim control. Worse, many crusaders, familiar now with the taste of blood and violence, robbed, raped, and pillaged the war-torn areas. In fact, even before the first Crusaders set out for the East, they stopped first in the Rhineland, where they murdered ten thousand Jews, according to Nakashima Brock and Parker, "nearly a third of the Jewish population in Europe." (271) This continued the long-standing "Christian" practice of killing "the other" in the name of God.

A Spiritual Hierarchy

By this time, patriarchy in Christianity had created a very hierarchical church. Clerics were the only ones who were allowed to interpret the Scripture for others. They could impose judgment on those who didn't agree with them and condemn them to hell. Since most ordinary people were not educated or even literate, they were seen by the hierarchical church to be ignorant sheep waiting to be told what to do. But what the people were told sometimes bore little resemblance to the example of Christ. Jesus preached compassion, love, mercy, welcome, care of the poor, making no distinction between male and female, free and slave, rich and poor. Preaching during the Middle Ages often strayed far from this Christian message.

Unfortunately, despite the widespread education that exists today, many people still give over their spiritual authority to gurus, clerics, or anyone else in power. I've often heard people say that they believe in a certain idea or principle just because their priest, minister, or whatever guru, political or religious, said it. They can't really explain the idea or principle, but that's okay with them.

This "sheep mentality" shows itself today especially on social media, where people often believe whatever they read, fact-based or not. "I found it on the internet" becomes a claim to authority. It's sad, really. I guess we've had centuries to learn this behavior.

Enter the Mystics

And yet, in the midst of all this trouble and indoctrination, then and now, the green thread of the Holy Spirit continues to weave life and beauty in the world and in the church. In fact, many people outside formal religious power positions have emerged to claim their spiritual authority amidst a Christian setting that denigrated their wisdom. And many times, those people have been women. Nakashima Brock and Parker report, "As scholars of religion have noticed, women who are excluded from male-dominated church leadership often gain authority through charismatic power granted by the inspiration of the Holy Spirit, usually via ecstatic visions and dreams." (72)

The period of the late Middle Ages highlighted an example of this reclaiming of spiritual authority. Even as the church was often engaging in aggression, and focusing on sin and punishment and blame of others, there were always people who embraced God's message of love and peace intimately. They *knew* and *felt* that they were loved for who they were, and they preached the oneness and goodness of all creation. These people are often called "mystics." Their spiritual authority was based on a personal relationship with God rather than just book knowledge.

Mysticism is not relegated to only certain types of people. All of us have probably experienced God in nature, in love, in beauty. A gorgeous sunset, a rainbow, a glimpse of fall leaves, their child's face, a dream, a vision, silence—all can reveal God to the person experiencing it. This is how I often experienced God. This, too, is mysticism.

Dorothee Sölle remarks that children often experience mysticism, this at-oneness with God and the world. "There are for many of us—I almost want to say for every one of us— moments of heightened experience in childhood in which we are grasped by a remarkable, seemingly unshakable certainty. Mystics in various ages have called upon this buried experience." (11) Can you unearth your buried mystic? Sometimes all it takes is to give yourself permission to watch a sunset, or take a walk in the woods, or watch your baby sleep. How could we deny a loving God in those moments?

Trusting the Inner Experience

Too often, when we tell others that we experienced a mysterious and powerful connection with God, they don't believe us. We know the experience happened, but we are taught not to mention it. So the memory of childhood mysticism often lies dormant, hidden under the overly rational mores and beliefs of church and society.

Richard Rohr, Franciscan priest, author, teacher, and founder of the Center for Action and Contemplation in Albuquerque, says this:

> Most of organized religion, without meaning
> to, has actually discouraged us from taking
> the mystical path by telling us almost exclu-
> sively to trust outer authority, Scripture, tradi-
> tion, or various kinds of experts . . . instead of
> telling us the value and importance of inner
> experience itself. . . . In fact, most of us were
> wrongly warned against *ever* trusting our-
> selves. Roman Catholics were told to trust the
> church hierarchy first and last, while mainline
> Protestants were often warned that inner
> experience was dangerous, unscriptural, and
> even unnecessary. (1–2)

It is true that the Crusades were an ugly episode of the church's focusing on violence and control rather than the example of Jesus. Yet, we can never underestimate the power of the Holy Spirit to bring about new life in the midst of darkness— our green thread. As the official church increasingly empha-sized religion based on doctrines, a number of people who had direct experiences of God's love, so-called mystics, refused to be quiet, much to the annoyance of powerful clerics. They preached the message of oneness and a loving God, and often wrote about their experiences, their dreams, and their visions, and distributed them to others.

The Saxon Mystics

Interesting to me, given the focus of my research and my personal path to healing, was my discovery that the former Saxon homelands became a center of growth for mystical spirituality during this time. I can't help but wonder if the Saxons' persecution under an unyielding patriarchal church eventually and ironically led to the release of some of their own mystical energy. Even before the Crusades, in the late tenth century, just two hundred years after Charlemagne's massacre of the Saxons at Verden, a woman named Hrotsvitha of Gandersheim became known as a mystic. Believed today to have been a member of the Saxon nobility, Hrotsvitha wrote many volumes of spiritual poetry and moral dramas, which were distributed to the people.

Later, in the thirteenth century, three women mystics from the northwest Germanic lands became quite well known. All three of them—Mechtild of Magdeburg, Mechtild of Hackeborn, and Gertrude the Great—were associated with the abbey at Helfta. The most famous of these Helfta mystics, Mechtild of Magdeburg, spoke and wrote in a Low German dialect, revealing her journey toward God and critiquing corruption in the church.

Laura Swan, a Benedictine sister and writer on the history of women's spirituality, observes: "When challenged by corrupt clergy, Mechtild claimed God as her authority for writing. On numerous occasions, she was threatened with the burning of her work, and she told her followers that as she was facing this threat, God consoled her by reminding her that the truth cannot be burned by anyone, for no human is stronger than God." (146) These German mystics provided people with an alternate way of perceiving and worshipping God.

Hildegard's Greening

Arguably, the most notable woman mystic from northwest Germany in the Middle Ages was Hildegard of Bingen. I have a special place in my heart for Hildegard, because that was my mom's name (though she spelled it with an *e* at the end).

Hildegard was born in 1098, while the First Crusade was in progress. She was forced by her mother at the age of eight to be walled up for life in a small set of rooms attached to a men's monastery. At the time, this practice was seen as making an offering to God. It also was believed to present an option for girls when prospects for a suitable marriage were scarce. Hildegard lived with a teenage girl named Jutta, who was consumed by fasting and self-denial, often punishing her body, an accepted path of the spiritual life at that time.

Mary Sharratt, in her well-documented and fascinating novel titled *Illuminations: A Novel of Hildegard von Bingen*, tells us that Hildegard was inconsolable as a child, as any child would be in these circumstances. She experienced visions from God at an early age. Now, in her new situation at the monastery, these visions became a consolation, as God revealed to her a view of the world very different from the orthodox theology of the time. She realized she was loved by God, and began to understand that Jutta's way of denigrating herself in order to become close to God was wrong.

In her tiny walled courtyard, as she grew to adulthood, Hildegard could glimpse the sky, the sun and the moon, birds, and the tops of trees, and there she also experienced God. She relished nature and often spoke of *viridatus*, meaning "the greening of things." As time went on, she began to grow herbs to flavor their food and use as medicines for the monks. She translated this deep understanding of plants into a recognition of the deep connection between God and the entire created world. In this view, everything is seen as one. This tradition, sometimes called creation spirituality, was also honored by the Celts, Francis of Assisi, Indigenous people throughout the world, and is practiced by more and more spiritual seekers today.

As a teenager and an adult, Hildegard learned to read and eagerly devoured all types of learning, eventually becoming a prolific writer, speaker, composer, musician, poet, prophet, and pharmacist. In her mid-twenties, she was pleased to be put in charge of the new girls who eventually came to join her and Jutta. Upon Jutta's death, Hildegard assumed the leadership of her small community. As soon as she could, Hildegard moved the group to a new convent in a nearby town.

In her thirty years walled up with Jutta, Hildegard had allowed her yearning for freedom, her love of nature, and her mystical relationship with God to build a solid core within. In this way, she claimed her spiritual authority. After that, she was not afraid to write and speak about God's love and the oneness of all creation. In time, she developed a large audience. Frances and Joseph Gies, authors of many books on the history of medieval Europe, have this to say about Hildegard:

> Many important people, both clerical and lay, wrote to her, and soon she was conducting a busy correspondence that ultimately included four popes, two emperors, several kings and queens, dukes, counts, abbesses, the masters of the University of Paris, and prelates. . . .
> Her tone in correspondence was that of an equal, if not a superior. (84)

It is not surprising, given all this, that many church officials saw her as a threat. Nor is it surprising that those in power began to seek out ways to silence her. As Anthony M. Stevens-Arroyo, scholar of religion and Puerto Rican and Latino studies at Brooklyn College, notes, "If direct Earth Religion experiences clashed with the written word as interpreted by the elites, authenticity could be questioned and the self-styled prophet might be cast out as a heretic, thus preserving the status quo." (5–6)

Hildegard was harassed by many of the monks from her old monastery, abandoned by some of her sisters, and was even brought up on charges of heresy by the church. In the end, however, she had enough allies to save her. Her large following of ordinary people rejoiced.

Remembering Hildegard of Bingen

Unfortunately, Hildegard and other women mystics from the Middle Ages were not in their lifetimes officially recognized by the church for their wisdom and holiness. In fact, they were in large part eventually forgotten by the faithful. But again, the Holy Spirit was not to be denied.

In our present day, Hildegard has become an important spiritual figure for people worldwide. In 2012, the Catholic Church finally acknowledged her spiritual contributions and named her a Doctor of the Church: someone whose doctrinal writings have special authority and are considered true and timeless. She is one of only four women ever given that title, the others being Saints Teresa of Avila, Catherine of Siena, and Therese of Lisieux.

Hildegard, the two Mechtilds, Gertrude, and their fellow mystics—many of whom were men, including the famous mystic Meister Eckhart, born in 1260—were able to be a green thread of life and resilience in a church that had become increasingly more rigid, dictating what was true and suppressing anyone who spoke from direct spiritual experience and authority from God. Is there a lesson for us to learn here? I think there is. When we reclaim our true spiritual authority from God, we are then able to challenge church and governmental authorities when they stray from their true callings, and lift up the wisdom and goodness of ordinary people.

Grünthrad, her eyes bright, is eager to engage. "You should know," she says, "that I heard my descendants talk about Hildegard. When they were feeling sick or bereft, they would search her out. They would travel long distances on foot, on horseback, or by raft on the great river you know as the Rhine. Even though she belonged to the Catholic Church that had conquered us Saxons, she was different. She treated everyone with respect and saw that they were good. That was something my people were often lacking. It was so wonderful! She used herbs and the methods of healing we women had used in the days we were free. My descendants could identify with her. Some of our young women even went to live with her. It seemed like a much better future than what otherwise awaited them."

"I understand what you are saying," I say. "Though the church has long suppressed memories of Hildegard, people in my time have reconnected with her. They, too, just like your descendants, look to Hildegard for guidance and spiritual inspiration."

"That is wonderful to hear!" exclaims Grünthrad. "I never thought that the old ways would be respected again. It makes me feel better, hearing that all was not lost."

"Yes," I reply. "But there were many things that bothered me as I wrote this chapter. One was how the church at that time regarded your menfolk as pawns."

"What do you mean by that?"

"Well, it seems to me like the church saw only one side of them, the fact that they were fierce warriors, and then used them to kill and maim. That must have destroyed their souls

and hardened them. And in the process, they undoubtedly learned that real men need to be aggressive and never show their feelings. Unfortunately, that sentiment is still important for some men today who are afraid of losing their power."

"I saw that same devastation in Odullieb when he was gone for a long time fighting wars," Grünthrad responds. "There was something missing in him when he returned. It made me so sad."

"There is something else that bothered me," I say. "It was that the church didn't teach your people true Christianity, who Jesus really was. It didn't teach you how loving and compassionate he was and ask you to model him. It only taught your people that Jesus was a warrior Jesus. What a terrible shame!"

"Thank you for telling me these things," says Grünthrad. "I had no idea."

12

Adopting a Third Way: Franciscans and Beguines

From the eleventh century on, Europe changed rapidly. What was once a highly structured feudal society—that is, a society based on land ownership that is controlled by a ruling class—now evolved into a society with a growing merchant class. Universities popped up, and Benedictine monks provided learning and structure. Educated clerics began to systematize Christian beliefs even further. This systemization of theology involved fierce debates among theologians, with the losers often ordered to recant their arguments or face excommunication.

One huge debate from these times, which has impacted Christians like probably no other, is the controversy over why Christ died on the cross. In the late eleventh century, Anselm, who was the archbishop of Canterbury and a theologian, put forth an argument to answer that question in his work called *Cur Deus Homo* (Why God Became Man). Nakashima Brock and Parker explain.

Anselm believed God would punish human
beings and bar them from heaven unless they
had performed sufficient penance to fulfill
their debt to God for their personal sins and
their sinful nature. Humanity's level of debt for
sin, however, was beyond any human capacity
to repay it. Nonetheless, unless it was paid,
none could enter heaven; all would go to hell.
To override this double bind, God paid humanity's debt. He became incarnate in Christ
Jesus to die on the cross, offering the gift of
his death to pay for humanity's crimes. . . .
[Because of this teaching] Christ's resurrection
became irrelevant. Anselm fails even to mention it in *Why God Became Man*. (267–268)

Anselm's theory became widely accepted in Europe,
and eventually became known as the atonement theory or
the fall/redemption belief. It has been the prevailing view in
Christianity ever since, and as Richard Rohr comments, "has
often been called 'the most unfortunately successful piece of
theology ever written.'" (184)

In fact, the atonement theory has led to an emphasis in
Christianity that actually undermines Christ's message.

The Gospel in Reverse

Again, Nakashima Brock and Parker offer an analysis: "Instead
of mourning the Crucifixion once a year and marking the
Resurrection daily, the Resurrection slowly receded in importance. Resurrection had no place for Anselm in salvation because the only purpose of the Incarnation was to accomplish

a saving death." (269) This belief is still very present to many Christians today, resulting for them in too much focus on sin and death and not at all enough emphasis on the joy of the Resurrection.

In my childhood, the Stations of the Cross—the physical prayer in which the priest or individuals would walk around praying in front of images depicting the stages of Jesus's suffering and death on the cross—included only fourteen stations. These stations ended with Jesus being laid in the tomb. Here again, the Resurrection was not even mentioned. Only after the Second Vatican Council in the 1960s did the church add a fifteenth station commemorating Jesus's Resurrection. But popular preaching and belief still often seem to favor death over Resurrection. This is a gross misinterpretation of Jesus's life.

Fortunately, many theologians today, especially those who work out their theology in the light of the experiences of groups on the margins, argue vehemently against the atonement theory. These theologians ask questions like: What happened to the love of God for humanity? Why is God depicted as a sulky child who is offended because humans make mistakes? Why is the cross emphasized over the Resurrection?

In my healing journey—as I came to love myself more and as I began to see God as the source of love and compassion, and not of judgment and harsh punishment—I found that this atonement theory made no sense and was even offensive to me. It undermined God and placed human beings in a terrible position—one in which they saw themselves primarily as sinners and were stuck in that definition. If you remember, this is the situation that leads to shame: seeing oneself as so flawed that one can no longer trust one's own goodness. People who believed the atonement theory had to rely on clerics to show them the way to avoid hell.

Back when I was deciding to go to Loyola University Chicago to get my master's in pastoral counseling, I knew that the degree paired psychology and theology. I looked forward to the study of psychology, but I didn't know if I could claim the theology they would teach there. So I met with one of the directors of the program and told him of my journey to reject the patriarchal theology of the Catholic Church. I didn't want to go backward. His reply helped me a lot. He said, "There are always different strands in the church." This statement gave me permission to explore my own understanding of my faith.

Lay Movements

As religious patriarchy and misogyny increased and many clerics became more corrupt in the twelfth and thirteenth centuries, lay movements—movements made up of non-ordained members of the church—that challenged these systems arose all over Europe. These lay movements, generally called *Vita Apostolica* or Life of the Apostles, promoted living the Christian life the way the original apostles and disciples of Jesus had: by sharing goods in common, serving the poor, accepting all as brothers and sisters, emphasizing the Resurrection of Jesus, claiming their spiritual authority, and having a direct relationship with God. These movements sought to bring back balance and wholeness to a church that had gone awry.

One of these movements was begun by Saints Francis and Clare of Assisi. Francis, the son of a rich cloth merchant, had loved to party as a young man. As he grew older, however, he felt the call to become a knight for God in the Crusades, a revered ideal of this time. Then after setting out for the battlefield, he was captured by the enemy. He spent a year in prison, and there he contracted a serious illness. While recuperating at home after he was released, he had time to really listen to and discern what God was asking of him. He realized he wasn't being called to be a soldier. Instead, according to Franciscan sources, God was asking him to "rebuild my church."

Being a practical man, Francis began to literally rebuild a church in the area of Assisi. Our ever-patient God then made the call clearer by telling Francis that he was to reform the Catholic Church, not rebuild a physical church. This work led him to a life of poverty, humility, and love of nature, all challenges to the hierarchical church. He famously embraced a leper and tamed the wolf of Gubbio, a wild animal that had been terrorizing an Italian town. These two examples demonstrate his love of and willingness to accept "the other," that is, to embrace those who are not accepted by society, those considered "not us."

Author Robert Ellsberg says this of the legacy Francis left us:

> Saint Francis, after all, was the saint who set out to rebuild the church by evoking the example and spirit of the poor man, Jesus. Saint Francis spurned violence and privilege. He reached out to members of other religions. He cherished the earth and all its creatures. He pointed to a new form of human and cosmic community, marked by love and mercy. And he did all this with a spirit of joy and freedom. (*Give Us This Day*, October 4, 2023)

How I long for the fulfillment of Saint Francis's dreams and ideals in today's world.

Clare's Rule

Clare, a young noblewoman of Assisi, wanted to literally follow Francis in his life and work, but as a woman, she was required to accept the enclosure of a convent. Still, even within the walls of the cloister, Clare embraced his practice of poverty. This went against the common practice in women's religious life at the time, when the convent depended on rich benefactors who had a huge influence on the life of the convent. Instead, Clare and her Franciscan sisters, now known as Poor Clares, depended totally on God and begged for what they needed.

Clare developed a contemplative life for herself and the sisters of her order. She taught them and others a fourfold method of prayer: Gaze upon Christ, contemplate Christ, consider Christ, imitate Christ. At the end of her life and after decades of her pleading with the pope, the church accepted Clare's rule, which she had written. This rule for a religious order was the first written by a woman to be accepted by the church and the first to enthrone poverty as a key element.

The Franciscan Way

The Franciscan movement also included single and married men and women. While these followers didn't enter the Franciscan religious communities with vows, they met in groups on a regular basis to pray and support each other in living the Franciscan way of life in the world. The Franciscan way was able to bring about change in the church from the inside, using no oppositional energy. Richard Rohr explains.

> [The Franciscan movement] found a way to be both very traditional and very revolutionary at the same time by emphasizing practice over theory. At the heart of their orthopraxy was the practice of paying attention to different things (nature, the poor, humility, itinerancy, the outsider, mendicancy, mission

> instead of shoring up the home base, and
> the Gospels "without gloss," as Francis put
> it). . . . They also de-emphasized other things
> (big churches, priesthood, liturgy as theater
> instead of prayer, ostentation of any kind,
> seeking church offices, hierarchical titles and
> costumes). (87–88)

These alternative views often left Franciscans in the minority position in the Catholic Church and in Christianity. But the Franciscan tradition continued to influence many in the church, both then and now.

One of the most famous Franciscan theologians was a man named Duns Scotus. Born in Scotland in the middle of the thirteenth century, he became involved in the great debate I mentioned earlier, about why Jesus had to die on the cross. Scotus did not agree with Anselm's atonement theory that said God had to be appeased because of our sins. Rather, he believed that God planned the Incarnation from the beginning. In Scotus's view, the Incarnation wasn't a reaction to human sinfulness; it was a way to proclaim God's great love for the world.

Scotus's theology makes so much sense to me. In fact, it has become one of my foundational beliefs. But, unfortunately, the majority in the Catholic Church sided with Anselm's theory, and has emphasized it to the present day. Franciscans, however, have tended to believe and to preach that the Incarnation was always in God's plan.

Beginning the Beguines

Another lay movement, this one made up of women of all ages and classes, first emerged around the year 1200 in northwestern Europe and northern Italy. Eventually called Beguines, the

French word for "true lovers," they emerged at a time when European society was changing. As the Crusades continued unabated for almost two hundred years and many men were lost in the violence, the roles of women began to change. They had to assume much of the work previously done by men, like farming and blacksmithing, and thereby they gained a new-found independence. Many of these women subsequently flocked to the cities in order to earn a living. They especially gravitated to the textile industry that was flourishing in Germany, Belgium, the Netherlands, and northern Italy. There they did spinning, weaving, and embroidery.

Some of these women desired to live a more spiritual life-style along with other women. Though some lived with family members, others pooled their earnings to buy single or group homes near the parish church, so they could gather to pray and attend Mass. Sometimes they eventually took over whole neighborhoods.

Beguines were quite comfortable with the new market economy. They owned their own homes, paid taxes, and were self-supporting. This both earned the respect of city leaders and gave them the freedom to pool their money to help the poor. They eventually established infirmaries, almshouses, hospices, schools for girls, and houses for lepers.

They, similar to participants in other lay movements of the *Vita Apostolica*, began to claim their faith in a deeper way. The Beguines followed no formal rule of life like nuns did, and the local bishop had no more say over them than over any other laypeople. Previously mentioned Laura Swan explains.

> Women began stepping outside the stric-
> tures and confines inflicted upon them by the
> church and the prevailing culture, seeking
> to express their faith as they felt called to
> it. They sought out preachers of their own

choosing, secured informal copies of the Bible
that existed in the vernacular and learned its
texts, and began experimenting with ways of
literally imitating the lives of the first apostles. . . . Beguines forcefully embraced the call
to holiness as *every* person's journey and not
just that of professional "holy people," namely
priests, monks, nuns, and others in formal
religious life. (13)

Beguines also were very involved in the new literacy movement sweeping Europe. While women couldn't attend the
universities that were gradually emerging, these independent
women invited academics and preachers to their own homes.
Along with other increasingly educated laypeople, they demanded better preaching from clerics as well as general church
reform.

Some of these Beguines began to write about what they
knew of God, often in their own languages, which went against
the norm of using Latin. Their groups then diligently copied
these documents and spread them far and wide. As you can
imagine, this didn't sit well with church authorities. According
to Swan, "Powerful medieval men were insulted by the presence of women living independent lifestyles and thus publicly
derided them. How absurd were these women to think that
they could live without the guidance of a father or husband or
cleric? How could women be trusted with their own spiritual
journey?" (11)

The Beguines were often accused of heresy, lewdness, and
promiscuity, and at times were even burned at the stake for
heresy. Multiple church councils over a period of three hundred years discussed how to control them. Such harsh punishments are typical misogynistic tactics employed within
patriarchal systems that are perceived to be under siege, with

people either asserting that women are stupid and easily guided into falsehood, or that they are whores, brazenly flouting the laws of God. We hear similar arguments today.

At the same time that the Beguines were meeting so much resistance from church authorities, there was a lot of support from their fellow citizens, nuns, and even some very powerful clerics. These supporters recognized the good work that these women were doing and admired their courage in proclaiming a return to Gospel values.

Ironically, support for the Beguines often increased in times of censure. The church engaged in many clashes with kings and princes over who had control. The church punishment for these wayward officials was often a censure known as an "interdict." Being issued an interdict meant that the laypeople of that realm were denied access to their priests, and therefore access to Mass, the sacraments, preaching, and even burial in sacred ground.

Interdicts could last for months or even years and were extremely difficult for the people to cope with. But interdicts also provided the Beguines an opportunity to use their spiritual authority. As Swan comments, "[I]nadvertently, the repetitive imposing of interdict encouraged beguines to exercise the pastoral ministry that the official church was withholding: preaching and teaching and leading informal prayer gatherings. Beguines filled the spiritual void created by an order of interdict, and thus their popularity grew." (161)

A New Way

As we have now observed, men and women, like the Franciscans, Beguines, and mystics, persisted throughout the many challenges of the Middle Ages, holding to a personal relationship with God and encouraging people to claim their own spiritual authority. They remained part of the church but challenged its boundaries. They became a green thread giving hope to many. Dorothee Sölle, referring to mystics, says this:

> The orthodoxies that have been handed down to us in the monotheistic religions called for obedience to the commanding God. They threatened with punishment and enticed with rewards—images of hell and heaven resting on that authority. . . . Mystical perceptions and approaches to God, however, are entirely different. . . . [T]he commanding Lord becomes the beloved; what is to come later becomes the now; and naked or even enlightened self-interest that is oriented by reward and punishment becomes mystical freedom. (36)

These women and men mystics that Sölle cites used their own deep relationships with God to offer people a new way of experiencing God and themselves. In doing this, they modeled what spiritual freedom and joy felt like. And their followers, in turn, were able to find the spiritual authority they needed to help others.

Grünthrad comes to me with longing in her eyes. "I wish I could have known your Francis of Assisi. He sounds like a compassionate man who treated everyone with respect. That is something we never encountered from our Catholic conquerors. They treated us like beasts!"

"I agree," I reply. "That is what bothers me so much! The Catholic Church, before it went astray, hopefully would have introduced you to the poor man, Jesus, and his disciples, who preached love and mercy and accepted everyone."

"So, that Jesus would have accepted us Saxons? He would have seen our lives as good?"

"Yes," I assure her. "He would have loved you unconditionally and seen the goodness in you. In fact, he still does. We Christians believe that Jesus lives yet through his Spirit. I can imagine that he is thrilled with your love of Mother Earth, your dependence on the Divine, and your strong bonds of community."

Grünthrad breaks out into a big smile. "I am beginning to accept that Christians were, and are, not all bad. And I can see that you follow your father Francis and Jesus, the poor one."

"Thank you. And I also model my religious life on the Beguines. They were strong women who were faithful to God their Beloved, and were not afraid to challenge patriarchy."

Grünthrad says, "I see that in you."

13

Nature, Women, and the "Other" Under Attack

The thirteenth and fourteenth centuries in Europe ushered in another blow to the balance in church and society, one that reverberates to this day. Beginning in China, and spreading to India, Persia, Syria, and Egypt, a deadly disease eventually made its way aboard sailing ships to the European shore. Once this plague struck land, it moved fast, killing huge numbers of people and coming back in waves every few years over a span of decades. What would later be called the Black Death is believed to have killed between one-third and one-half of the population of Europe.

We in the twenty-first century can identify with the horror of a pandemic. We have seen death and sickness all around us; we have experienced isolation, distrust, fear, despair, and a deep urge to make sense of what life and survival mean. Unfortunately, we often lacked the resources to cope with this unimaginable devastation. Even though we had the medical resources our ancestors lacked, many of us lashed out at the very people and organizations that were providing some relief. Concerns for our own well-being and battles over politics often kept us from having the collaborative working relationships that were desperately needed. Both the government and the church often failed to step up, except to bury the dead. People felt abandoned.

Grappling with a Plague

The people and the church in the thirteenth and fourteenth centuries similarly felt abandoned. They tried to make sense of the meaning of the plague they faced, but life-giving spiritual resources for doing this necessary inner work were lacking. The only resources the church could offer them were the beliefs and the doctrines that emphasized a sinful humanity, a judgmental God, the holiness of suffering, and an emphasis on a better life in heaven. These "resources" just made matters worse. The only answer they could find to relieve their hopelessness, anger, and the burden of their trauma was to blame the plague on others.

We know how to do that too. We in the twenty-first century United States also tried to make sense of our pandemic by blaming others. "It can't be our fault. We are good white people trying to obey laws. Those 'others' must be to blame." The "others" we scapegoated—our targets varying depending on our beliefs or our political or social position—were numerous: Asians, Africans, pro- or anti-vaccine proponents, the poor, migrants, transgender people, Democrats or Republicans, Jews, people of color, and on and on. The ways we scapegoated and lashed out were as numerous and far-ranging as the variety of scapegoats themselves—people engaging in social-media lies and smear campaigns, high government officials spreading falsehoods about different groups, other people screaming at each other out in the world, or committing assault and even murder. Our frustration was so great that probably all of us at some point let loose our aggression on others. We didn't know how else to cope.

The people of the Middle Ages lived in more homogeneous environments than we do, so the number and types of scapegoats available to them were fewer in number. They had long focused their criticism, as critics always tend to do, on Jews and women. But now in the time of the plague, they added a new group to scapegoat—heretics. A heretic is defined as "a professed believer who maintains religious opinions contrary to those accepted by their church or rejects doctrines prescribed by that church." (dictionary.com) Due to the increasing number of individuals and groups who were rightfully challenging and criticizing the church during this time, clerics felt that they were under siege and began to see heretics everywhere.

"Heretics" Everywhere

This reaction became a mania, infecting the population with fear and anger. Bishops, rulers, and even local mobs began to accuse, prosecute, and punish people who were seen as sinning against God and endangering the community. Often these charges were false, but the so-called heretics were punished anyway.

Through the years that followed, the papacy involved itself more and more in fighting heresy. Official investigations by the church, or inquisitions, were instituted around 1232. Members of the male Dominican order were tasked with the responsibility to oversee these tribunals of intense questioning and investigation. Many of these Dominicans were well-educated men who saw this as their religious duty and tried to be fair. But others were unfair and ruthless.

During this period in the thirteenth century, some heretics were burned at the stake. Although the state was okay with this, the church had not officially approved this punishment for heretics at the church-sponsored inquisitions. But then Pope Innocent III decided that heresy, a church matter, should be equated with treason, a state matter. This, in effect, made it a crime against church and state to believe anything different from official doctrine. Consequently, succeeding popes authorized the burning of heretics, thus making the death penalty an official church policy.

At War with the Natural World

Eventually, this persecution of heretics widened its focus to people who employed gifts of the natural world to heal. Remember, at the time of the Saxon annihilation, trees and other forms of nature were already viewed as suspect, considered part of pagan belief. Now, with the devastation of the plague, people didn't know who or what had caused it. They felt helpless and needed to blame someone or something.

Nature can be very mysterious and seen as dangerous, so nature as a whole became the enemy and needed to be actively attacked. As the priest and theologian Matthew Fox states in *Julian of Norwich: Wisdom in a Time of Pandemic—and Beyond*, "As it transitioned from loving nature to fearing it, humanity shrunk its soul and came to see itself in a battle *against* nature." (xxi) Unfortunately, this distrust of the natural world has persisted to this day in Christian practice, giving rise to the human impulse to control and subdue nature, one of the many factors leading to the climate crisis we are now facing.

Blame Falls to the Witches

Once the hierarchical church turned against nature, it likewise was apt to turn against women. And this it did. Women had always been more associated with nature, the wild, the uncontrollable, what with their rhythmic cycles following the moon, menstruation, childbirth, and their involvement in caring for the sick and dying. Clerics often saw these processes as very mysterious and uncontrollable, and therefore dangerous. They were seen as something to fear.

During the fifteenth through seventeenth centuries, the search for heretics expanded even further into the prosecution of witches. The word "witch" comes from the Old English word "wicce" meaning "female sorcerer." Long ago, both old and young women healers were often called witches. They used their knowledge of plants, the seasons, and the human body to heal their community members. These women claimed their personal and spiritual authority and brought new and valuable information and practice to their communities. But the patriarchal system couldn't abide anyone who routinely failed to obey the hierarchical rules. So witches began to be seen as evil, and they were accused of consorting with the devil and leading others away from the true church. The institutional church believed that they had to be hunted down and punished.

I have found *The Oxford Handbook of Witchcraft in Early Modern Europe and Colonial America*, edited by historian Brian P. Levack, to be a great source of information on witchcraft. In it, the historian Thomas Robisheaux states that, although this hunting of witches took place in many countries of Europe and North America, "the German lands have long been known as the 'heartland of the witch craze.' Of the estimated ninety thousand individuals prosecuted for witchcraft in Europe, at least thirty thousand and possibly as many as forty-five thousand came from the [German lands]. . . . Approximately twenty-five thousand of an estimated fifty thousand legal executions for witchcraft took place within the lands of modern-day Germany." (179)

These statistics help me to understand what was happening to and around my ancestors in northwest Germany. The victims were mainly women, especially women who had claimed their spiritual authority. But the effects of these persecutions went beyond punishment of the victims. A spirit of distrust, scapegoating, and violence began to infect these small communities of farmers. People in once-close communities began to distrust everyone. Struggles between neighbors and disagreements over proper behavior often turned deadly.

But why was Germany such a center for the persecution of witches? According to multiple articles in the *Oxford Handbook of Witchcraft in Early Modern Europe and Colonial America*, witch trials tended to take place mostly in areas that lacked stability—socially, politically, and religiously. Where people felt unsure, desperate, and chaotic with little leadership to calm them and restore trust, they tended to get paranoid when more misfortune happened to them. They looked for someone to blame, and this time it became witches who were seen as bringing evil into the communities. I can't help but compare this situation to that of the US and beyond today. We, too, are experiencing chaos. Whom are we blaming today? Who are our witches?

A Climate of Uncertainty

During the Middle Ages, what we now call Germany was a very splintered land. There were probably about two thousand semi-independent principalities, duchies, lordships, abbacies, and cities all under the overall authority of the Holy Roman Empire. But this empire was a rather weak institution. In the absence of strong leadership, the various local governments often fell into local feuds, infighting, and disputes among neighbors.

In addition to this unrest, the climate played a large part in compounding the tension and uncertainty experienced by farmers in northwest Germany. The Little Ice Age, which hit Europe between 1560 and 1720, brought about lower annual temperatures, longer winters, heavier rainfall, and shorter growing seasons, which all resulted in smaller harvests, famine, and disease. This suffering caused more anger, desperation, and a search for someone to blame.

Many scholars have noted the correlation between agricultural tensions in communities and the surge in witchcraft trials. Robisheaux explains.

> At the height of the [witch] trials between the 1580s and 1630s, witches were often accused of weather magic, spreading toxic powders on fields, and poisoning domestic animals and people. (182) In addition, community and religious norms governing marital and communal behavior—with their emphasis on obedience, deference, harmony, piety, restraint in speech, dress, and decorum—could make women who seemed repeatedly to violate such norms vulnerable to accusations of witchcraft. (192)

Older women and widows were especially vulnerable to such accusations. These women were often wise, independent, confident, well-off, and claimed their spiritual authority, which threatened the male authorities. Though we rarely now call a strong woman who claims her spiritual authority a witch, such a woman still threatens patriarchal authority today.

Kathe Schaaf, whose roots are in northern Germany, gives a personal example that reveals how her own spiritual heritage as a woman was severely impacted by Christian imperialism.

The through-line of my spiritual heritage
took a very different turn when Christianity,
patriarchy, politics, and economics converged
to rain down upon the old religions of Europe.
A series of events [including witch burning]
spanning hundreds of years resulted in
successfully severing those spiritual threads.
Women took the brunt of this assault. . . . It
was enough to silence the voice of feminine
wisdom, to sever women from their natural spiritual authority, and to leave most of
Europe with a God defined and described
only as masculine. (226–227)

Julian's Creation Spirituality

One person who tried to right this imbalance was Julian of
Norwich (1342–ca. 1415). Norwich was a town in England
that had been settled by Anglo-Saxons, the cousins of the Old
Saxons. Julian was a young girl of seven in 1347 when the Black
Death first struck her hometown. It kept returning in waves
every few decades throughout her entire lifetime. Who could
be more justified than she to place blame on nature? But she
rejected all this negativity. Instead, she focused on the goodness of life and creation.

Julian lived her life as an anchoress, that is, a woman who
lived walled up in a small cell attached to a church. She had
a window out to the street and was thus able to interact with
people and experience the horror unfolding outside. Because
she was enclosed and primarily alone, she had a lot of quiet
time to ponder deeply and pray about what was happening in
the world. Through prayer and revelations from God, she came
to know a loving God who abides in all people and in nature.

In her writings, she urged people to come to know this God and abandon all false ideas of a God who focuses on sin and punishment.

As Matthew Fox explains, Julian truly claimed her spiritual authority.

> A singular characteristic about her writing is that in her books she cites very few theologians or even biblical texts. Having learned to integrate her readings thoroughly into her own thinking and with years of contemplative study, she creates her own theology. She learns to trust her own experience, especially the revelations themselves, and she spends decades following her first book, unpacking them for the wisdom they contain. . . . In doing so, she creates a fresh theological vision and invites the reader to participate by trusting their own experience. (xxx–xxxi)

Julian also wrote extensively about the divine feminine, God as mother. She saw a one-sided patriarchy as lacking a full sense of God and what the church could be. She called people to a sense of oneness, to a healthy balance and wholeness. Julian's emphasis on creation spirituality, the oneness and sacredness of all creation, and seeing God as both loving father and loving mother was so needed at the time of the Black Death, just as it is today.

Julian's way of spirituality would have been very helpful to people as the church became a source of divisions and veered away from a balanced view of the world. But most people in the church never knew about Julian's creation spirituality until recent times. Now they are rediscovering this wise woman.

The green thread of hope continues to prevail. This wise

woman consoles us with one of her most famous quotes from her book, *Revelations of Divine Love*: "All will be well. And all will be well. And every kind of thing shall be well."

This is my question: Do we have the courage to believe her?

Grünthrad begins, "I saw my people suffer through the Black Death. It was horrible! And it went on for a long time. Even worse, some of my kinfolk who had preserved some of the old ways were blamed for it. Our conquerors were always looking for ways to keep their power over us by blaming everything on us and our beloved Mother Earth."

"I suspect patriarchal conquerors have always been like that," I reply. I pause before I go on. "But what really bothers me is that persecuting and executing heretics, especially women, became an official policy of the church. Institutionally, it was deemed okay. This church, which I always loved and always wanted to serve as a good Catholic, betrayed all of us by the use of this kind of ruthless power! I saw it in history, but now I see it play out in modern times, too, albeit in different ways. I guess I never realized when I was younger what an ingrained institutional problem this quest for power and control had become."

Grünthrad seems perplexed. "This doesn't sound like the ways of the Jesus you told me about. I thought you said he loved all of us, and that his followers were to do likewise. This makes me think that the church would have accused me of being a heretic and killed me, too, if Charles had not done it sooner."

"I don't have a good answer for that," I bemoan. "All I can say is that the hierarchical church got lost for a while."

14

The Age of "Discovery"

The intense suffering and unrest in Europe led many people to believe that the world was coming to an end. And again, just as it had been in the tenth century, the hierarchical Catholic Church was at a loss for ways to help and console. Its clerics taught that God was punishing the people, and individuals were encouraged to atone for their sins through devotional practices like fasting in the extreme, flogging themselves, and undertaking arduous pilgrimages. Obviously, none of this consoled the people. It just piled more suffering on top of their current suffering.

After the tenth and eleventh centuries, devotional images of Jesus and the martyrs became more and more bloody as the church glorified suffering for Christ. Where was the hope? Making the suffering even worse was the fact that paradise at the end of all the suffering on Earth was not guaranteed by the church anymore. In 1274, the Second Council of Lyons established the doctrine of purgatory, which said that sinners (everyone) would spend time after death purging the sins they had not atoned for before death. Now even paradise was not assured.

Everywhere there was more suffering. Consequently, more and more people began to look for a way to escape it. Some turned to exciting tales of beautiful faraway lands abounding in riches, real paradises on Earth, like those in the reports of the explorer Marco Polo and in a collection of fables that told the story of Prester John. According to Nakashima Brock and Parker, he was a mythical, rich Christian king living in a vast land somewhere unknown, watered by rivers of paradise, who, in these widely circulated stories, invited people to join him. (317) Others, most of them men, literally found a way out.

Men on a Mission

In the fifteenth century and thereafter, many adventurous men set out to look for the "New World" and its riches, men like Prince Henry the Navigator from Portugal, Vasco de Gama, Cristobal Colon (Christopher Columbus), and others. These explorers were usually supported and financed by the riches of Catholic monarchs and popes. Whatever wealth was taken from the conquered lands was then fed back into the coffers of these sponsors.

The purpose of these missions was not to bring the love of Jesus to groups that were already recognized as civilized. In fact, the papacy and the adventurers saw all these "foreign lands" as "wild" with "savages" inhabiting them. European Christians believed it was their duty to subjugate these peoples in order to civilize them and save them for Christ. The Europeans believed that they, and only they, were the settled and advanced civilization. Little did they understand that many of these "wild" lands already had civilizations much more highly developed than those of Europe.

As Peter Brown, professor of history at Princeton, states, "In a process which lasted over half a millennium, from around

AD 400 to around 1000, Christianity came to hold the center. It came to stand for the world of order. It came to be identified with the world of human settlement as defined in sharp contrast to the wild." (485) Again, Christian imperialism raised its ugly head. Christian leaders wanted to control the world.

Watching for Evil

Peter Brown has put forward a unique idea. As Christianity evolved, he argues, the northern European concepts of the world and of theology began to shape what had been wholly Mediterranean views in earlier days. For example, for Christians in southern Europe, the conceptual model of evil or demons was a vertical model. Demons were seen as spirits that threatened from above: fallen angels who could invade or control a person and cause much destruction. But the belief was different in northern Europe. Brown explains.

> What we meet in the north, by contrast, was a more horizontal model. Evil did not come from the sky. It was not "demonic" in that strict sense. It came across the open land, and it was utterly concrete. We are dealing with a patterning of social imagination which saw settled human society as surrounded, on every side, by the encroaching wild. A "middle world" of human order was forever hemmed in by an "outer world." (482)

This argument makes sense to me because I can imagine a clan sitting around a campfire as protection from the northern winter dark and cold. The fire was not only protection against freezing to death but also protection against the wild beasts who could attack them. That was a constant threat. So, for northern Europeans, anything or anybody outside their inner circle was looked on as a threat of evil.

It seems to me that in patriarchal theological doctrine and theory today, the Mediterranean view holds sway. In patriarchal Christianity, the war between angels and demons is constantly being waged, and Christ is the militaristic figure who will vanquish the demons. But when it comes to living the Christian life, too many people seem to endorse the northern view, thinking that anyone outside their group or clan is dangerous and must be persecuted. When you combine these beliefs, Christian nationalism can be the result, as we have seen. Those who see themselves as the "true" or "real" Americans or Christians think they need to protect themselves from the rest of the world all around them, which they feel is in various ways dangerous.

The Doctrine of Discovery

In the latter part of the fifteenth century, many kings and queens, as we have seen, were sending their adventurers to discover, conquer, and convert the "pagan" lands. This practice was officially endorsed by the Catholic Church through a series of papal "bulls," or edicts, written between 1445 and 1494. Collectively, these edicts came to be known as the "Doctrine of Discovery," and this period became known as "the age of discovery." In 1455, Pope Nicholas V issued the papal bull called *Romanus Pontifex*. Matthew Fox describes its scope and implications.

> [It] extended to Catholic nations of Europe
> dominion over discovered lands during the age
> of discovery. It encouraged the enslavement of

native and non-Christian peoples in Africa and
the New World. Calling the king to "invade,
search out, capture, vanquish, and subdue all
Saracens and pagans whatsoever, and other
enemies of Christ wheresoever placed, and
the kingdoms, dukedoms, principalities,
dominions, possessions, and all movable and
immovable goods whatsoever held and possessed by them and to reduce their persons to
perpetual slavery." Thus the global slave trade
of the fifteenth and sixteenth centuries and the
age of imperialism were buttressed with ecclesial backing—all of it in the name of a religion
of redemption. (116)

This document was to have dire consequences for much
of the world, causing deep trauma to people all over the globe,
including in the land that would become the United States.
Actually, the United States was established and built on this
Doctrine of Discovery. From the beginning of our history, we
condoned the mistreatment of human beings, causing untold
harm and destruction to the land's Indigenous people. Martin
Luther King Jr., in *Why We Can't Wait*, echoed this truth.

Our nation was born in genocide, when
it embraced the doctrine that the original
American, the Indian, was an inferior race.
Even before there were large numbers of
Negroes on our shore, the scar of racial hatred
had already disfigured colonial society. (119)

Much of this imperialism was tied into the "Christian" belief system of the times. As you may remember, these European
conquerors believed in the atonement theory (explained in

chapter 12), as unfortunately too many Americans still do today. They saw the people they conquered as savages who needed to be redeemed. As Fox points out in his book on Julian of Norwich, "The doctrine of discovery promotes original sin in spades—original sin institutionalized, frozen, and projected onto all 'non-believers.' It served as the primary instrument in denouncing the primal religions of humankind. Without Christian redemption they were doomed—in this life *and the next!*" (118)

How sadly ironic—most of these Indigenous peoples who were subjects of this "saving campaign" already had a deep relationship with the Divine. They well understood the sacredness of nature and the oneness of all creation. They were in fact surrounded by the goodness of their gods, and they thanked their divine beings constantly for all the blessings given to them. It seems they had a lot to teach these so-called Christian colonizing powers, but they weren't given a chance.

To make matters even worse, this Doctrine of Discovery was not just a doctrine of the church; it also found its way into the public international arena of so-called Christian countries. For example, in 1823, it was used by the United States Supreme Court, and continues to be used even in recent times, mainly to support decisions invalidating or ignoring Indigenous possession of lands in favor of colonial or postcolonial governments' imperialism. The result is that both church and government became allied *again* in keeping the "other" in check. This has devastating consequences for all of us.

James A. Houck Jr. argues as follows:

> [F]or all our feeble attempts at sanitizing
> human history, blood spilled in the name
> of murder, genocide, Manifest Destiny,
> cover-ups, the Doctrine of Discovery, slav-
> ery, forced starvation and encampments,

> lynching, and exterminations, to name a few,
> are still evident in both the land that holds the
> energy where blood was shed, as well as the
> souls that remain ensnared there. As stated
> earlier, these phenomena are especially true
> when such violent crimes against humanity
> were committed in the name of God. (5)

Can you see the parallels with the harsh treatment of the Saxons in the ninth century and beyond to our treatment of Native Americans, African Americans, immigrants? And this harsh treatment continues.

A Spiritual Revival

Despite this dark history, the Spirit of God remains among us, weaving a green thread of life and healing into our lives. In the worst situations imaginable, there have been, and there continue to be, people and groups motivated by this grace to speak the truth and exemplify the love and mercy of God. Ironically, it was the innovations and progress in the world outside the clerical church in medieval times that brought the ordinary people the means to again access their spiritual authority.

In the fifteenth century, the German Johann Gutenberg pioneered movable type, which allowed the same typeset to be used again and again. Before this invention of the printing press, manuscripts had to be laboriously copied by hand by monks and nuns. But now new writings could be multiplied rather quickly. Soon more and more people were able to own books. Subsequently, demand for books written in the varied languages of the people increased.

The first large book printed on the new printing press in 1456 was the Bible. Now ordinary people had personal access to the Scriptures without a cleric having to explain them. They could read what was actually written and then use their own intelligence and spiritual authority to recognize how these scriptures impacted their own lives.

Another trend that inspired the ordinary person to claim their spiritual authority was the explosion of beauty in the building of the great cathedrals. Real beauty awes us and is often a way that God speaks to us and in us. I suspect you know this experience of awe and inspiration firsthand. Such beauty takes us beyond ourselves to deeper truth and goodness. In addition to being a source of beauty, the images in the stained-glass windows of the cathedrals also told stories from the Scriptures, which was very helpful to people who might have been illiterate. Now they could personally discover the meaning of Scripture in their lives. The cathedrals also became gathering places for the communities, often serving as meeting spaces for the guilds or sleeping space for poor pilgrims.

Also at this time, the rise of new universities not associated with monasteries offered education for laymen, at first just for those who wanted to be priests. But eventually universities taught, besides theology and philosophy, courses like mathematics, science, medicine, and law.

In all these ways, the mysterious ways of the Spirit continued to bring forth life and to open avenues of opportunity for ordinary people to become better, to embrace their strength and resilience, to understand themselves and the world around them. Doing all these things helped them to make their own conscious decisions about what God was asking of them.

As a result, in the late fourteenth century, a new spiritual movement called the *Devotia Moderna* or "the Modern Way of Serving God" began in northern Europe. Philip McNair, formerly professor of Italian at the University of Birmingham, England, describes it this way in Dowley's *Introduction to the History of Christianity*: "This was a spiritual revival that began within the Catholic Church . . . and strongly emphasized both personal devotions and social involvement, especially in education." (300) More and more ordinary people were inspired to embrace the message of Jesus.

As we have seen, there were many ways that laypeople gained strength and spiritual authority in the fourteenth and fifteenth centuries and beyond. But despite these threads of hope and empowerment, the hierarchical Catholic Church had reached a new low. When the fifteenth century began, there were two popes serving at once, and eventually even three, each man challenging his rivals at every turn. Corruption and infighting in the church were constant, with many of the clerics concerned only with power. Women and men of conscience realized how bad things were, and began to urgently press for reform.

One of those people seeing the need for reform was Nicholas of Cusa (1400–1464). Nicholas was a cardinal in the church from the German territories in addition to being a philosopher, theologian, diplomat, mathematician, and astronomer. Even centuries before the church recognized the authority of its laypeople, Nicholas was already writing on the importance of balancing hierarchy in the church with consent from the people. In addition, he showed a tolerance of other religions (even though he still saw Christianity as superior).

All of this supports the idea that this was an "Age of Discovery," though in a different way from how the term was first intended. As we have seen, many people "discovered" their strength and spiritual authority in the midst of very difficult times. I am beginning to see that many of these people with newfound authority came from the German lands. I believe that it was the inner resilience and strength of my Saxon ancestors that prevailed, and this belief gives me hope.

I am ready to rant. "I keep thinking about the phrase I quoted from Matthew Fox in this chapter: 'The age of imperialism [was] buttressed with ecclesial backing—all of it in the name of a religion of redemption.' The white Christian rulers, both papal and political, saw themselves as the rightful rulers appointed by God to convert the savages and pagans—that is, everyone but themselves—at any cost. That is so wrong!"

Grünthrad responds in surprise. "You are really angry today! I've never seen you like this before." Breaking into a smile, she says, "Now you sound a lot like me!" She goes on. "It seems we have both been awakened to the real harm that was done to us by imperialistic patriarchal Christian rulers. This seems like a first step in healing our trauma—to recognize it."

"I agree. The more we know, the more we can discover what we need to do to address it. But it is so hard!" After an uncomfortable pause, I continue, "I have something to tell you. It is very difficult for me to say, but I need to." I look down for a moment. "I believed our rules and thought you were a bad person who needed saving. That is, you and people like you." Again, it takes me a while to get myself together. "Remember how I told you that in grade school, we students would bring in money to convert pagan babies in foreign countries. We believed that pagans were being raised to believe terrible things. We were brainwashed to believe that we were your saviors, since we were better than you and had the right beliefs." I look directly at her and say, "I am so sorry! Now that I know you, I realize how good you are and how devoted to the Divine you are. I am ashamed and humbled."

Grünthrad replies, "Well, this is hard to hear from my own descendant! But I am grateful you could say it. This understanding will hopefully deepen our relationship. And that's what I want."

"I do too."

15

Reform and Reaction

Morally, the Catholic Church of the Middle Ages limped into the sixteenth century, having been radically altered by patriarchy, misogyny, clericalism, and Christian imperialism. While there were many clergymen who were faithful and compassionate toward their people, there was also rampant corruption among others of the clergy, involving sexual abuse and immorality, financial misdealings, negligence, and absenteeism. This corruption was often ignored by members of the hierarchy, who were more focused on gaining power and wealth themselves.

Philip McNair provides a stark description in Dowley's previously referenced *Introduction to the History of Christianity.*

> Never had official religion been at a lower
> ebb, or the public image of Christianity more
> defaced, than in the second decade of the
> sixteenth century. It seemed as though all op-
> position to the unreformed Catholic church
> from within and without was dying away. . . .

[But] in October of [1517], in an obscure
province of the empire, one roused German
conscience was stung into protest—and the
great revolution began. (303)

That "roused German conscience" belonged to Martin
Luther (1483–1546), a professor of biblical studies at the
University of Wittenberg. While he was a loyal Catholic,
Luther was also very aware of the many abuses in the church.
One particular abuse that he understood needed correcting
had to do with the punishment for one's sins.

The church had now introduced the belief that purgatory
was the usual precursor to heaven. In purgatory, people would
suffer to atone for their sins, albeit temporarily. But "tempo-
rary" could be a long time. Unscrupulous priests and laymen
took advantage of people's fear and began to sell something
called indulgences, that is, instructions on ways to reduce
punishment for one's sins. Buying indulgences promised to
shorten a person's time in purgatory.

Martin Luther was appalled by this practice. In Dowley's
book, James Atkinson, formerly director of the Centre for
Reformation Studies at the University of Sheffield in England,
puts it this way:

Luther saw that the trade in indulgences was
wholly unwarranted by Scripture, reason, or
tradition. It encouraged people in their sin,
and tended to turn their minds away from
Christ and God's forgiveness. At this point
Luther's theology contrasted sharply with that
of the Church. The pope claimed authority to
"shut the gates of hell and open the door to
paradise." An obscure monk challenged that
authority. (305–306)

Indulgences were still a practice when I was a kid, as was the belief in purgatory. Money was no longer charged for indulgences, but we would be asked to perform a penitential task in order to gain the removal of some allotted amount of time in purgatory for ourselves or our friends and family. I can remember praying in church three Our Fathers, three Hail Marys, and three Glory Be's to gain an indulgence. A person could gain only one indulgence per visit. It was funny and sad at the same time to see people go in and out, in and out, in and out of church multiple times in order to gain as many indulgences as they could in a short amount of time. They surely felt relieved when they left, knowing that they had lessened their time in purgatory.

This practice always seemed ridiculous to me. At some level, I think I realized that a loving God would bestow love and mercy on people no matter what. But at another level, I had been taught that God was a judgmental God. So I, too, would say the triad of prayers one time. If the church said it worked, I figured I might as well hedge my bets and gain at least one indulgence. This is yet another example that illustrates how we laypeople were told that we were basically sinful, and therefore we couldn't believe that God actually loved and forgave us in this life.

Luther Speaks Out

In 1517 Luther stated his theological argument against the abuse of indulgences through a list of ninety-five theses that he nailed to the door of the parish church. In doing so, he was inviting others to join him in a sincere discussion of the theology of indulgences. He wasn't planning on leaving the church. This is a great example of someone claiming his spiritual authority and reaching out to others so that all could gain deeper enlightenment together.

At first, the pope and the emperor disregarded this action. After all, it was just one person. They were both busy in their search for power, wealth, and esteem. But Luther didn't give up, and as he wrote and spoke more about the scandal of selling indulgences, more and more of the Germanic people took note, and found themselves agreeing with him. Atkinson proclaims, "Luther's dramatic stand against both pope and emperor fired the imagination of Europe." (306) Finally, the pope and the emperor realized the extent of the brewing challenge to authority that Luther presented. After a number of meetings with papal authorities over two years, Luther was asked to recant his views on theology. But he refused. As a result, he was excommunicated in 1521.

Luther continued to publish his views in many books over the next twenty-five years, written in German and not Latin, so that the ordinary people could read the arguments for themselves. Luther's movement, or Lutheranism, spread throughout the Germanic lands. According to Atkinson, "Almost the whole of north Germany and nearly every German free city was on Luther's side." (313)

The theological split between Lutheranism and Catholicism also caused a deep political divide in the Germanic lands because of the close connection between church and state. Armed conflict and persecution between the forces of Catholics and Lutherans erupted for many years. Finally, in 1555, both sides agreed to the Peace of Augsburg, which allowed each local ruler to determine the religion of his own domain.

On one hand, this agreement resolved some of the conflict. But, in effect, it once again split the already splintered Germanic lands, and ordinary laypeople were forced to embrace the religion of whoever was their ruler. This left many feeling bewildered and spiritually suffering after the religion that they had believed in and practiced for countless years was haphazardly denied them without any input from them. It is difficult to claim one's spiritual authority when others are telling you what to believe and practice.

Most of the local rulers in the north chose Lutheranism, while those in the south tended to choose Catholicism. Looking at a map of the former Saxon homeland (northwest Germany) in the 1600s shows mostly Lutheran territories with a few Catholic domains. This division remains much the same today. My ancestors were mainly from two of those Catholic enclaves, Paderborn and Oldenburg. Surrounded by sometimes-hostile Lutherans, Catholics drew into themselves by becoming more and more self-sufficient and suspicious of strangers.

New Catholic Reform

During this period of change, the official Catholic Church began at last to recognize that some reform of the church needed to happen. Pope Paul III, who reigned from 1534 to 1549, was instrumental in attempting reform. His most important contribution was to call an ecumenical council (a gathering of all church leaders). The Council of Trent, called this because its venue was the town of Trent in northern Italy, met in three sessions between 1545 and 1563.

The Council of Trent reaffirmed most of the doctrines that were under dispute by the Lutherans. It also defined Catholic teachings in a more comprehensive way, and it set new rules for establishing order and eliminating corruption in the church. One of these decrees stated that Christian faith is based on the Bible but also in the tradition of the Catholic Church. This decree reinforced the belief that the Catholic Church had the final word on how to interpret the Bible. It also continues to cause problems for ecumenical dialogue to this day as it sets the Catholic Church above all other authorities in the interpretation of the Bible.

After the council sessions, a number of resources were published by the Vatican to make sure that the beliefs reinforced at the council would be believed and practiced by Catholics everywhere. Among these resources were a standardized missal, a catechism or summary of church teachings, and a list of forbidden books that were said to oppose the teachings of Catholicism. According to Robert D. Linder, this index, published in 1564, "censored nearly three-quarters of all the books that were being printed in Europe at this time." (423) The list was updated periodically until 1966 when it was finally abolished.

The above rules remained in place when I was growing up, four hundred years later. On one hand, Catholics were proud of the fact that we could go to Mass anywhere in the world and it would be the same. But memorizing the catechism didn't really help me to deepen my faith. It was basically a rote exercise. The only things that were important were that we believed that the church authorities knew better than we did, and that what we were parroting was the truth.

Of these rules mentioned above, the banning of books has particularly struck a negative chord with me since we are again experiencing this in our present day. Again, people who think they know the truth about what's moral and what isn't, or who are pushing their own political agendas, are trying to rob all of us of our spiritual authority. I am grateful that many people today realize this and don't let it dictate their actions.

With the various storms assailing it—like the Protestant Reformation, the increasing emphasis on individual freedom, and scientific explanations for phenomena that were previously claimed by the church to be strictly spiritual matters—the Catholic Church after the Council of Trent found itself initiating what came to be called the Counter Reformation. Linder explains as follows:

There arose a new Roman Catholic piety and

> a better-defined Roman Catholic orthodoxy.
> The Council of Trent and the leadership of
> reform-minded popes provided a solid basis
> for this new piety and renewed orthodoxy.
> The beliefs of the Church of Rome were
> better understood, even by the rank and file,
> and differences between Roman orthodoxy
> and Protestant doctrine now stood out more
> clearly. (358)

Unfortunately, in taking back its power and authority, the church set up even more of an "us vs. them" situation. Everything and everyone that challenged the Catholic Church's authority was condemned. The hierarchy doubled down on proclaiming that only the Catholic Church possessed the truth, and that the laypeople did not have the tools to read and interpret Scripture.

This claim of exclusivity led to more tension within the Catholic Church and with non-Catholic denominations, as could be expected. In addition, various other Protestant groups soon differentiated themselves from Lutheranism, but they were not recognized as legal religions in the German territories, and were thus often persecuted by the government. What ensued was the Thirty Years' War (1618–1648). It began as a conflict in Germany between Catholics and Calvinists (another religious group formed at the time of the Protestant Reformation), but eventually was joined by German Lutherans, Danes, Swedes, and even the French, as all sought territorial control in Europe. The war ended with an agreement called the Peace of Westphalia, which essentially stated the same thing the Peace of Augsburg had stated one hundred years earlier: Each ruler could determine the religion of his land.

A Broken Germany

Peace had come, but the war had taken a terrible toll on Germany. Six million people had died, yet another reminder to the people of the great losses suffered during the Black Death. And once again, the church was unable to provide consolation and hope to the survivors.

At the time, the Mass was essentially distanced from the people. In the large cathedrals, the ordinary worshippers were made to watch from afar as a "communion rail" literally separated priest from people. The priest celebrated Mass with his back to the people, and in a language most people could not understand. The Eucharist was considered the holiest of holy rites, and laypeople were not seen to be as holy as the priest was. Seeing the host raised during the consecration was all they could expect. Receiving Communion was something they usually did only once a year. This situation left the people feeling distant from God.

Thankfully, even in the midst of such suffering, ordinary people stepped up to exercise their resilience. This is the green thread we have seen so often. In this case, resilience showed up when the people began to rely on their hearts and souls instead of dogma alone for their spirituality. Since the people saw God and Jesus as distant, they began to express their faith through pious devotions to the saints with whom they could identify. The people asked saints to intercede for them with God in heaven. The Blessed Mother, Mary, was particularly honored with devotion, shrines, and special feast days.

In this way, people were able to embrace a more personal spirituality that touched their lives and brought them peace and comfort.

Grünthrad begins, "I've been thinking about the things you have been writing. Through the many years that my spirit has been endlessly roaming the earth, especially in my homeland, I have become aware of all the ways my kinfolk tried to protest against Christian tyranny. Because it was dangerous, much of this protest was in little things. But you have been naming many of the Saxon descendants who were the first to step out and plead publicly for new ways of thinking and doing things. I noticed that Martin Luther received most of his support in his protests from the people of my home territory. This support even caused most of them to leave the Catholic Church."

Considering this, I muse, "I could very well have ended up being a Protestant. But because the territories where my ancestors lived were ruled by Catholics, all the inhabitants had to accept the Catholic religion. This was so random! Just like your Saxon people, we were not given a choice about how we worshipped God. This realization gives me a better understanding of what your immediate family went through when they had to give up their nature religion."

"I am happy that you can understand," replies Grünthrad. "We both need to grieve this assault."

"And to think that all the violence between religions could have been averted if the Catholic hierarchy had been more vulnerable and more willing to dialogue," I bemoan. "The hierarchy, in their arrogance, believed that they were God's chosen and, therefore, could do no wrong. People who disagreed with them were accused of heresy."

"It sounds like more of the same," Grünthrad says.

"*I agree,*" *I tell her.* "*This division between religions contin-ues to this day. In my growing-up years, I experienced the divi-sion between Catholics and Protestants, just like the division between them in Germany. We were quite insular in our small Catholic town. Now I see the larger picture—divisions between Catholics, Protestants, Jews, Muslims, Indigenous religions, and many more.*" *I grow quiet, considering, then cry,* "*Aren't we all worshipping the Divine?*"

"*I wish it were that simple,*" *Grünthrad muses in resignation.*

16

Revolution

The seventeenth through the nineteenth centuries was a time of revolution in Europe. Ordinary people had been through centuries of Crusades, plagues, witch burning, droughts, war, and oppression at the hands of whichever king or emperor or lord had conquered them. They were tired, discouraged, and angry. They sincerely wanted something to change, and they began to dream that things could be better for them. Many became empowered and began to fight for their rights and their freedom. For example, in 1776, the North American colonists declared independence from England. In 1789 a group of French peasants attacked the Bastille, a Paris prison, releasing all the prisoners and eventually destroying the building. This led to the demise of the French monarchy.

Other revolutions rippled across Europe, both between ruling governments and their constituents and between the church and civil rulers. In addition to all that was the beginning of the Industrial Revolution in Europe, a period in which societies shifted from producing most goods by hand to making them by machines. This shift changed work as people knew it. It brought new wealth and opportunity for the factory owners, but it led to many abuses of the workers.

Increasingly, the Age of Reason and Enlightenment brought forth philosophers who argued for political, religious, and personal liberty. Everything that had been taken for granted for centuries now came under attack. Consider the example of rationalism. According to Carl Koch, director of spirituality centers and author of several books on spirituality and church history, rationalism was a philosophy that held that "the universe was regulated completely and reasonably by universal natural laws that could be explained by science. According to the rationalist perspective, people did not need the Bible and religious authority as sources of truth." (216) Some people with this perspective even went so far as saying that God did not exist.

In this changed environment, doubt and skepticism of authority figures and institutions began to prevail. New ways of thinking and the resultant popular movements—such as nationalism, rationalism, liberalism, secularism, capitalism, empiricism, and individualism—alarmed and challenged the church and the various political rulers. As so often happens with new movements, these shifts ignited a strong reaction from those who wanted to retain the old ways and their power. Instead of being open to a new world in their midst, the Catholic hierarchy again closed ranks. All that was not approved of by the official Catholic Church was considered wrong and punishable.

Galileo the Heretic

A famous example of this mindset is how the church dealt with the Italian astronomer and devout Catholic Galileo Galilei. As you may remember from your school days, Galileo believed and helped scientifically prove that the earth travels around the sun, not the other way around. Many people of the time did not believe that this could be true, including leaders of the official Catholic Church. Koch reveals the results of this discomfort:

> Unfortunately, the church condemned Galileo's findings as heretical. But Galileo's dedication to scientific truth never shook his faith in God, in the truths of the Bible, or even in the church that condemned him. He, like Isaac Newton, saw the discoveries of science as compatible with religion, not as contradicted by religious truth. (217)

Galileo was forced to recant his theory and placed under house arrest by the church. Fortunately, the truth finally prevailed. In 1992, on the 350th anniversary of Galileo's death, Pope John Paul II apologized for the church's error. It was realized that there is no opposition between science and faith. Once again, it took a very long time for this to happen.

Chaos of a Changing World

At this point in history, the Catholic Church was also split internally between the conservatives, who wanted to strengthen the rule of the pope and the rules and regulations instituted at the Council of Trent, and the liberals, who wanted the church to change in order to meet the needs of the world and to get laypeople more involved.

For example, in Germany in 1763, the Catholic bishop of Trier, J. N. von Hontheim, wrote an opinion that led to a movement named Febronianism. Wayne A. Detzler, a professor of biblical studies and missions, noted in Dowley's book that von Hontheim, writing under the name Justinius Febronius, "argued that the keys of the kingdom of God had been committed to the entire church, not only to Peter and his successors. Consequently, the church councils, not the pope, were the primary source of authority." (429) This opinion spurred a nationalist and spiritual movement in Germany that the official church strongly opposed, though by then, many people had already come to recognize that they had spiritual authority and could challenge the church hierarchy if necessary.

The world at that time was in chaos, much as it is in the twenty-first century. In such times, rulers often use uncertainty and chaos to assert unilateral power and control. We see this happening around the world today.

During the eighteenth and nineteenth centuries, Napoleon Bonaparte of France was such a leader. First, Napoleon seized control of the French state in 1799. He brought about some reforms, but his ultimate goal was to control all of Europe. His imperial ambitions led him to war with the papacy and with much of Europe, where he conquered lands, including the Germanic lands, and people. Napoleon was finally defeated by the British-led allied army in 1815, leaving destruction and death in his wake. Teva Scheer, author of several books of historical nonfiction, describes in *Our Daily Bread: German Village Life, 1500–1850* the dismal aftermath of Napoleon's wars.

> [1816] was remembered in history books as
> the Year Without a Summer, when cold and
> damp destroyed crops and people rioted
> for food across Europe. . . . Compounding
> the series of poor harvests, troops from the
> recently ended Napoleonic wars had, over the
> last several years, been confiscating what little
> food the villagers had been able to grow. To

> pay for the wars, the villagers were forced to
> give more than half of their harvests in taxes,
> in addition to their usual burden of rents,
> tithes, and fees. (1)

The revolutions that continued to sweep Europe brought chaos and dismay to many long-established institutions, Detzler says. "[As a result,] many of the continent's monarchs felt that their only hope lay in reasserting their divinely ordained rule and the authority of the church. At the Congress of Vienna in 1815, the great powers . . . showed their desire to carry on as though the Revolution had never happened." (429–430)

But many people refused to go back to the old ways.

An example of this refusal can be seen in the riots that broke out again in Germany in 1848, with the people demanding reform. As a result of the riots, the king allowed a representative assembly to take place in Frankfurt, which resulted in the publication of the Declaration of the Rights of the German People. It seemed that finally there was some progress, but it didn't last long. Three years later, the document was annulled, and everything returned to how it had been.

A Syllabus of Errors

The Catholic Church followed this example of extreme reaction to the new world. Wayne Detzler describes the results: "The events of 1848–1850 had instilled in [Pope] Pius IX a profound fear of the contemporary world; just as the European leaders of 1815 had tried to reverse the changes of the revolutionary era, the pope now reacted to the onslaught of liberalism by trying to turn back the clock." (434) One action Pius IX took was to issue the *Syllabus of Errors*, an all-inclusive list of errors that set Catholicism against the modern world. (434)

When growing up, I heard about the *Syllabus of Errors* but didn't really know what it included. I knew, though, that there were many things Catholics weren't supposed to believe or do. And I got the general sense that "Big Brother" was watching. This was just another example of fearmongering from the hierarchical church that I was accustomed to. I wish I could say that this fearmongering didn't bother me, but it did, since at that time I was still greatly influenced by this hierarchical church.

Pope Pius IX went even further by calling the First Vatican Council, which turned out to be a showdown between liberal and conservative Catholic bishops. The conservatives triumphed when the doctrine of papal infallibility was adopted in 1870. This doctrine taught that the pope is infallible (meaning, he can do no wrong) when speaking *ex cathedra*, or with the authority of his office, on matters of faith and doctrine.

Strong reaction to this assertion was quickly forthcoming. Some governments sent formal protests. The German Catholic Church historian Ignaz Döllinger expressed strong arguments against papal infallibility. When told to recant, he refused and was excommunicated, just like Martin Luther had been three hundred years earlier.

The Catholic Church and the Modern World

In the years following the First Vatican Council, papal successors made some attempts to reconcile the church to the modern world. However, the reactionary mindset of the official Catholic Church lasted for centuries, and still influences many Catholics today.

As we have seen, revolution is not usually welcomed by church and governments. But revolution does not always involve armed conflict. Sometimes revolution can be a green thread of life and hope.

For example, in 2018, my congregation of sisters, the Franciscan Sisters of Perpetual Adoration, met as a whole as we do every four years to discern our call to mission until the next assembly. At that time, we invited our lay affiliates, those people who pledge to live out the FSPA mission, to join us for part of the time to listen together for what God and the world were asking of us. I mention this because our theme for that three-day gathering was "A Revolution of Goodness." Some people, both inside and outside the group, were uncomfortable using the word "revolution" because to them it connoted violence and anarchy. Unfortunately, those features are often true of revolutions, but we sensed we were being called to another kind of revolution—a positive revolution.

An alternate definition of "revolution" is "an activity or movement designed to effect fundamental changes." At our gathering, we challenged ourselves to bring about radical change by promoting goodness wherever we encountered it. In this way, one revolution of goodness could have a strong impact on the world that too often focuses on negativity, blame, and violence. One of our affiliates remarked during that weekend, "It's so amazing that we can spend a whole weekend embracing goodness! Where else would that happen?"

Faith of Our Foremothers

In fact, our foremothers in religious life had already begun this type of revolution centuries earlier. Christian religious life for women has existed since the beginning of Christianity in one form or another, but most people don't know much about it. Jo Ann Kay McNamara, former professor of medieval history at Hunter College, explains this in her book *Sisters in Arms: Catholic Nuns Through Two Millennia.*

[The] impact [of this sisterhood] has been felt throughout the world but, against all reasonable evidence, monastic historians traditionally refused to see anything but their cloister walls and enveloping veils. Reasoning that women do not build institutions or conquer new worlds or make history, the scribes who shape the past have ignored their untidy existence or simply accorded it a hasty nod before pressing forward with the more readily accessible history of male institutions. (3)

And yet that sisterhood has persisted. It has gone through many permutations through the centuries, from the hermit "desert mothers" to groups of women who attached themselves to male monasteries for protection and support.

Gradually over the Middle Ages, European nobility established Catholic convents for their female relatives, especially in the tenth and eleventh centuries. McNamara states, "The German nobility was spectacularly active. Between 919 and 1024, it endowed at least thirty-six communities of women in Westphalia alone, dramatically outnumbering male foundations. Indeed, some tenth century Saxon families would not be known to us at all but for the lavish foundations of their women." (181) These were my Saxon ancestors! I am so proud of them.

Why would women even want to enter these convents? Frances and Joseph Gies explain.

For upper-class women, the convent filled several basic needs. It provided an alternative to marriage by receiving girls whose families were unable to find them husbands. It provided an outlet for nonconformists, women

> who did not wish to marry because they felt a
> religious vocation, because marriage was re-
> pugnant, or because they saw in the convent a
> mode of life in which they could perform and
> perhaps distinguish themselves. The nunnery
> was a refuge of female intellectuals, as the
> monastery was for male. (64)

The women leaders of these convents, supported and given legitimacy by their noble families, became very powerful, both in the religious sphere and civil arenas. I wonder if you can guess what happened next in an increasingly patriarchal church. You got it! The hierarchy felt threatened by the inde-pendence and power of these women. And, as always happens with patriarchy, misogyny and repression followed. Women were depicted as temptations to God-fearing clergy. Once again, just like in the times of witch burning, they were por-trayed as evil, promiscuous, and feeble of mind.

Then in 1298, Pope Boniface VIII decreed that all religious women must be cloistered—that is, they had to live in closed convents, separated from the world. In addition to cloistering, these convents were to be overseen by clerics, and each had to follow one rule of life written and approved by the hierar-chy. (Clare of Assisi was an exception. She wrote her own rule.) Women followed these rules, at least for the time being. But they would not do so forever.

A Women's Revolution

By the time of the great revolutions in Europe in the seven-teenth through nineteenth centuries, women religious were no longer content to remain in their cloisters, watching from a distance all the suffering of the ordinary people outside their convents. They felt that they were called by God not just to prayer and contemplation, but also to going out to serve the poor, the sick, the uneducated, and the workers in the new factories, much like the Beguines had done centuries earlier. They often had powerful allies in their priest spiritual directors who helped facilitate this change.

According to Carl Koch, one example of this new kind of religious life for women was the Daughters of Charity, founded by Louise de Marillac in the mid-1600s in France.

> [This] new group of sisters was revolutionary. [They] went out in the streets among the poor people, and they wore the style of dress of French peasant women. . . . Soon the Daughters of Charity ran hospitals, hospices, orphanages, and schools. (114)

Quickly, this revolution in religious life for women spread. As expected, many in the hierarchical church challenged this movement, and often were joined by other women who were complicit with the hierarchy. But more and more of the new religious orders for women combined prayer and contemplation with service to the poor and marginalized.

As the centuries went on, women religious continued to ask themselves, "What is needed in our church and in our world today?" Once women religious discerned a direction, they adopted ministries to meet those needs. Sisters became leaders in many church arenas, like Catholic education and health care.

As the late twentieth and early twenty-first centuries arrived, women religious expanded their collective voices, serving as lobbyists for Catholic social teaching, as social service workers, and as retreat and spirituality center directors. They have addressed homelessness and human trafficking, promoted care for the earth, and tended to migrants. Benedictine

Sister Joan Chittister challenged the leaders present at the 2006 annual meeting of the Leadership Conference of Women Religious, saying, "We must be those who live at the center of society to leaven it, at the bottom of society to speak for it, and on the edge of society to critique it." (LCWR National Assembly, August 22, 2006)

But no longer do women religious do this work alone. Today they embrace their roles as initiators, collaborators, inspirers, conveners, and participants with other mission-driven people, working together wherever they are needed to make the world a better place.

Not just women religious but all of us are called to a revolution of goodness—to recognize and promote goodness wherever we find it. As the cofounder of the Catholic Worker Movement, Dorothy Day, was quoted as saying, "The greatest challenge of the day is how to bring about a revolution of the heart, a revolution that has to start with each one of us." (Ellsberg, *Give Us This Day*, Nov. 29, 2024)

This is the challenge for all of us. This is the beginning of employing our spiritual authority to make the world a better place.

Grünthrad is excited! "Your words have energized me," she exclaims. "They give me hope. There are always good people, like your fellow sisters, who stand up to tyranny and persecution."

"Yes, they exist in every time and place," I say. "Often they just need support, education, and example from others to claim their spiritual authority." I take time to formulate what I am going to say. "But I am disturbed by the people who still believe that revolution for change must be put down by armed violence and trampling on people's rights. So many people in my country of the United States see that tyranny as their only option in stopping the change that needs to happen. They are afraid and give away their authority." I wonder aloud, "What lesson can your descendants teach me and others?"

Grünthrad replies, "At first, obviously we submitted. We were quiet. I recognize now, after our discussions, that all the while there was a deep desire to be free. When others began to voice dissent and desire for reform, it was often the former Saxons who rose up and proclaimed the truth, like Hildegard of Bingen and Dorothee Sölle. They banded together with like-minded people to initiate change. We have great strength and resilience in our family. I am proud of them, and of you."

"Thank you," I respond sincerely. "You have given me much hope."

17

Saxons Coming to America

The political, religious, and social upheaval in Europe in the mid-nineteenth century became a turning point for many Germans, including my Saxon ancestors. They had had enough of wars, military conscription, religious strife, crop failures, and lack of opportunity, and now they looked to a new life of freedom elsewhere.

One of the main reasons for emigration at this time was the growing landless class in Germany. The following is part of a report by scholars John Tholking, based in Cincinnati, and Josef Borgerding, based in northwest Germany. It was published in a 2012 *Tracer* magazine article titled "Vechta (Oldenburg)—Cincinnati Genealogy," which refers to the region of Vechta in northwest Germany, the very center of my family's origins.

> For over a thousand years, family farms, by law, were never divided. . . . Long ago it was realized that if a farm were to be divided among several children every generation, after many

generations there would be little land left in
one piece to sustain the farm. . . . The oldest
son usually inherited the farm and the rest of
the children could receive a share of household
items or money. Other sons either had to work
for the older brother, seek another respectable
profession such as a teacher or priest, or perhaps seek their fortune in the new world.

Many young men and women wanted their own land to
support themselves and start families. Increasingly, they began
to see America, especially the Midwest, as a shining beacon of
hope. There they could find flat, fertile land that was just like
the land back home, and perfect for farming. The US government was offering land to hardworking immigrants for $1.25
an acre, up to 160 acres. What a tremendous opportunity! And
so they went.

I must acknowledge that my ancestors likely did not think
about the Indigenous people who already lived on this wonderful land. By that point, it had become normal for white immigrants to believe that this had become their land, and that
it was therefore necessary to violently oppose any attempt by
the native peoples to reclaim the land they had inhabited for
ten thousand years.

As it turns out, my ancestors, even though they may not
have recognized it, were participating in the results of the
Doctrine of Discovery, that horrible power grab embraced by
the church and various governments, including our own. They
were acting in the same manner as Charlemagne had in the
eighth century. My family's own intergenerational trauma,
which they had forgotten, was leading them to inflict the same
trauma on our Indigenous sisters and brothers.

The German emigrants who came to America sent back
home glowing reports of their situations and asked their

family and friends to join them. And they did. According to Scheer, the first group of Germans to settle in North America consisted of thirteen Mennonite families who were seeking religious tolerance in Pennsylvania in 1683. Scheer reports subsequent developments.

> German immigration continued at a slow but steady rate in the United States through the 1820s, when an average of less than six hundred arrived in the United States each year. During the 1830s, however, the number increased to over twelve thousand each year. During the early 1840s, the number grew to over twenty thousand per year, and by the end of that decade, almost sixty thousand arrived yearly. During the early 1850s, the average annual rate was greater than one hundred thirty thousand. (162)

As I mentioned earlier, my ancestors were part of this migration, coming to the US between 1845 and 1874.

I found out through my research that most German immigrants tended to come in groups and joined family and friends who had already settled in the US, like my ancestors had done. This process is called "chain migration." The earlier immigrants helped to feed and support the new arrivals until they could get on their feet. They set up groups and associations to help their friends and families to find jobs, deal with government authorities, purchase land—whatever it took to get them settled.

German Culture in the United States

German immigrants also established other organizations to deepen their solidarity and culture as a group. According to

Stephen Szabados, an author and lecturer on genealogy, "Most German communities had a singing society, and some had dramatic societies that performed German plays. . . . Their doctors and lawyers formed professional organizations. The most important groups were the mutual-aid societies that provided sick and death benefits insurance policies. The societies usually were organized based on religion and place of origin in Germany. They provided a social gathering to bring together people of similar backgrounds." (161–162)

In fact, my hometown of New Vienna has one of these mutual insurance associations. It began in 1863 at a wedding, when the festivities were interrupted by calls of "fire." Bob Mescher and Laverne "Toby" Bockenstedt, in their book commemorating the sesquicentennial of Saint Boniface Parish and the centennial of New Vienna, report that the farm of one of the guests burned to the ground that day. The other wedding guests took up a collection to help the owner and his family. Then they realized that they, too, needed protection against fires. So, the pastor called a meeting to form the mutual insurance society.

At first, the society consisted of twenty-two members, all German Catholics and members of Saint Boniface Parish in New Vienna. Gradually it expanded to people of any religion and to five neighboring counties, and today covers a multitude of insurance needs. This is a great example of neighbor helping neighbor. I am proud to say that my great grandfather was an officer of the association sometime in the early 1900s, and my dad was its president in the 1980s.

Another important cultural heritage feature of these German communities was beer. Both the brewing and the consuming of it were long-standing practices from their home country. The people grew barley and hops on their farms, and then used the residue of the brewing process to feed their cattle and horses. Taverns and beer gardens were social centers for the community, serving men, women, and children not just beer but food and music as well. These were places where friends and families could mingle and socialize. My small Catholic town of New Vienna, with a population of around three hundred people, had a number of taverns and even had its own brewery for a while. It began in 1857 and operated until 1917 when it closed due to the upcoming Prohibition. (Mescher and Bockenstedt, 82)

In addition, as Szabados explains, the Germans preserved their culture in America through the publication of German-language newspapers.

> In 1851, there were about 89 [German-language newspapers in America], and by 1860, there were 144. . . . [T]heir main benefit was to inform their readers where new land and jobs were available. They also told their German readers about German merchants who could furnish them with items they needed and introduced them to American merchants who sought their trade. (163–164)

The work the German immigrants did to form tight social structures and self-sufficiency as a group probably was prompted from their experience in their homeland. At that time, each small Germanic territory was governed by separate rulers, and there was very little trade between various territories. This tendency toward self-containment was exacerbated by the Catholic—Protestant divide in Germany. Towns right next to each other often had very different beliefs, and the people of each one distrusted the people of the other, a reaction born of centuries of discord, persecution, and war. It felt safer to be self-sufficient and not depend on anyone else.

Anti-Immigrant Sentiment

These were the circumstances in which my ancestors came to America. As I mentioned earlier, within forty years of settling New Vienna, northwest German Catholic immigrants had bought up enough land around New Vienna to support eleven hundred families, so that they and those who followed them could live in close proximity to each other.

I didn't realize it before, but my research has since revealed to me that this acting on an instinct for group self-sufficiency by German immigrants alarmed many other Americans who had settled in our country much earlier. The following quote from the 1700s in Pennsylvania, another place where many Germans settled, reflects what many Americans in later centuries would come to feel about the immigration of Germans. Benjamin Franklin expresses his own views on the topic in an essay he wrote in 1755. "Why should Pennsylvania, founded by the English, become a colony of aliens, who will shortly be so numerous as to Germanize us instead of our Anglifying them, and will never adopt our language or customs, any more than they can acquire our complexion." (qz.com)

In a letter two years earlier, Franklin states that he wasn't against having the Germans immigrate since he recognized the virtues of the Germans—their industry, frugality, excellence as farmers, and their ability to improve the US. But his later essay also shows that he wanted them to be dispersed throughout the colonies in order to dilute their influence.

In addition to xenophobia, my immigrant ancestors encountered anti-Catholic sentiment. Carl Koch describes the situation.

> As the number of Catholics in the United States increased, the English-speaking, Protestant majority became afraid of the Catholic immigrants

coming into the country. Persons who called themselves nativists wanted the United States for "native-born Americans"—that is for themselves. . . . . Rumors and even publications by educated persons circulated claims that the Vatican and the Catholic immigrants were conspiring to take over the United States. (240)

What a shock it must have been for my Saxon ancestors who emigrated to America to realize that once again, they were discriminated against because of who they were! Trauma upon trauma.

Rise of the Know-Nothings

Eventually, in the 1830s and 1840s, this anti-Catholic, anti-immigrant sentiment coalesced into an activist group called the Know-Nothings. Following the recent demise of the Whig Party, these Know-Nothings formed a political party called the American Party, which tried to get their members elected to office on an anti-immigrant platform. This group became very active in Wisconsin because of the large German and Catholic populations there. But after the onset of the Civil War, this American Party melded into the Republican Party.

In the following years, Americans' focus remained on the divide between North and South, and anti-immigrant and anti-Catholic sentiments moved underground for a while. But they didn't die. Those old enough to remember resistance to the 1960 presidential campaign of John F. Kennedy may recall experiencing a déjà vu moment. At that time, the same rumors and innuendos from a century earlier spread throughout the country. The propaganda proclaimed that Catholics were trying to take over the country for the Vatican. However, amidst this propaganda, because of their close-knit communities, German immigrants seemed to thrive.

Saxon Descendants Prosper

With the growth in numbers of the German Catholic population, German bishops in the US realized the need for German religious sisters to minister to the needs of the pioneers in the Midwest, especially in schools and orphanages. Their pleas were heard, and many German women religious responded to the call.

Wisconsin drew many of these religious communities because of its large number of German settlers. My congregation, the Franciscan Sisters of Perpetual Adoration, came to Wisconsin in 1849 as a group of laywomen intent on forming a religious community and serving the needs of the Germans, which they did as soon as they could. We quickly established schools and orphanages and eventually hospitals.

Throughout all the ups and downs, challenges and setbacks, the former Saxon people prospered. Overall, Germans, through their hard work and communal support, were able to establish a firm foundation in the US. As Teva Scheer reports, "By 1900, a 'German belt' of German immigrants and their descendants extended across the center of the United States in an area bounded east and west by Ohio and Nebraska, north and south by Wisconsin and Missouri." (168) And again according to Scheer, in the census of 2000, Germans were still the largest ethnic group in the US. (4)

The Winds Shift

But, in 1917, the US declared war on Germany, and everything changed.

Now all Germans were under suspicion of being spies. They felt they had to prove their loyalty to their new country. Some changed their names and refrained from speaking German in public. Across the country, the things that had drawn them together earlier, like the German-language newspapers and the cultural organizations, began to disappear.

Specifically, in my home states of Wisconsin and Iowa, Germans felt the widespread distrust and often experienced harassment, as chronicled by Erika Janik in her article, "A Short History of Wisconsin."

> Some Wisconsin towns refused to teach German in their schools and German-language books were burned in Wisconsin streets. Indeed, anyone with a German name was a target for harassment; a widely published notice from the American Defense Society stated that a German American, "unless known by years of association to be absolutely loyal, should be treated as a potential spy." (119)

Iowa went even further. In 1918 the governor issued the Babel Proclamation, which proclaimed that "only English was legal in public or private schools, in public conversations, on trains, over the telephone, at all meetings, and in all religious services." (https://history.iowa.gov>education) Many Iowans took advantage of this moment to usurp the economic power that German-Iowans had gained. They undercut their influence in local, municipal, and state politics, and even harassed them for being German. Towns and institutions changed their German names so they wouldn't appear to be disloyal. Thank God, New Vienna was spared some of the atrocities inflicted on other Germans because of its insular nature. Almost everyone in town and the surrounding farms was

German, and consequently they were shielded from harassment in most cases.

Scheer reports the result of these changes: "By the onset of World War II a generation later, the golden era of German culture in North America was over." (169) The former Saxons had once again endured the annihilation of their culture as they did back in the time of Charlemagne. They no longer spoke of their ancestors from Germany. It was too dangerous. Many cut off all correspondence. The result was a loss of stories about who they were and what their lives had been like in their homeland. This is the same situation I encountered at the beginning of this book—*silence*.

Until I started researching this topic, I really had no idea of how German Saxon culture had been systematically stamped out in the US by people and institutions ruled by fear. I didn't realize what impact cutting Saxon descendants off from our Saxon heritage would have on us. I had no clear picture of the extent of my loss, which Thomas Hübl describes this way:

> Just as the condition of an individual's nervous system contributes to wellness or dysfunction, the health of our collective roots dictates how communities and societies respond and adapt . . . to change. Collective trauma, such as that caused by the communal scars left behind by war, acts as a great blade severing those roots, cutting us off from one another and from ourselves. It breaks our ties to home and homeland, abandoning us to the pain of isolation and the hamster's wheel of a denied past. (86)

I sense that some of this intergenerational trauma has stayed with us Saxon descendants in the US in the forms of retaining a victim status, being mired in shame and rage, needing to blame others, and looking to powerful men to save us.

What about you? Do you know how intergenerational trauma has affected you and your family? I hope that we all will find the courage to embrace our history, both the trauma and the resilience our ancestors have exhibited. This is the way forward to reclaiming our spiritual authority.

"I had no idea of what happened to my descendants who left for America," Grünthrad says. "I am so sorry that again you were subject to persecution." She speaks with great sadness. "Is this when you were forced to forget about me?"

"I guess it was," I reply. "I didn't know the impact this losing of your culture yet again might have had on you and my other ancestors. We abandoned you. And, in the process, we lost all the resilience, gifts, comfort, and inspiration you wanted to bestow on us. I'm so sorry—for you and for us."

"I lost track of you also," Grünthrad admits. "And that added to my despair. I felt so alone. And I was deprived of recognizing the good things that you and your relatives accomplished. As I said earlier, I felt no hope. It was awful! But now I am beginning to see that you did have resilience and used your gifts to make a difference in the world. Maybe I passed some of that down to you. Now I can feel proud rather than lost. We are family!"

"Yes!" I exclaim. "I am so happy that we have connected. Now the strength and resilience each of us has developed can flow back and forth to the other. I surely need it right now. My country and the world are in such chaos. I want to use my spiritual authority to speak out and give people the hope they long for."

Part Three

18

We Have Arrived

We have arrived. Yes, you and I have arrived at the third part of this book. In it, we will see that, although patriarchy, misogyny, and Christian imperialism are still alive, there are many people who are claiming their spiritual authority to counteract these dangerous forces. The Spirit is still with us, as always, providing us with resilience and wisdom to follow the green thread into new life.

We have arrived. Yes, we Saxons have arrived, as have you and your lines of people, and everyone else who has come to this land. We have all arrived from somewhere—all of us, that is, except for our country's Indigenous people who were, of course, already here.

Yes, we immigrants have arrived in the United States, the self-described land of opportunities, hope, and resources. The US has been good to some of us, *and* it has broken our hearts. Now we have arrived in the twenty-first century, and once again, as it has done countless times before, our country is trying to redefine itself. Make no mistake; it is a good thing for individuals, groups, and institutions to periodically assess their values and practices. But in this present time, trauma, isolation, and destructive political and religious movements have led us into chaos and polarization.

We are so divided, in fact, that it is hard to see a light at the end of the tunnel. Fear has taken over many aspects of our lives. We have hunkered down in our own little political and social bunkers with our own people, to keep the world at bay. And when we are not cowering, we are raging and blaming others. We are definitely living in trauma mode. Brian D. McLaren, a former pastor and now activist, public theologian, frequent guest lecturer, and core member of the Center for Action and Contemplation in Albuquerque, describes our collective situation this way:

> Centuries of crusader colonization have
> produced deep trauma that still inhabits the
> global human psyche, demon-like. This trau-
> ma expresses itself in internalized presump-
> tions of superiority and privilege among the
> descendants of the colonizers, along with
> an almost desperate obsession to remain in
> power, for fear, perhaps, that if they let up
> for an instant, the colonized will do to them
> in the future what their ancestors did to the
> colonized in the past. Among the descen-
> dants of the colonized, the trauma often
> manifests as a mirror-image presumption of
> internalized inferiority and hopelessness . . .
> or as an unending besiegement by lament
> and rage. (33)

Our Catholic Church is not exempt from this trauma and division. Catholics of my generation hoped it would be different.

Opening the Windows

As I entered high school in 1963, the Second Vatican Council was underway in Rome. We young people were so excited! I remember keeping a scrapbook with all the news articles on the council. Pope John XXIII had called this gathering to "open the windows and let in the fresh air." He wanted to break down the walls that had separated the church from the modern world for so long, ever since the Reformation.

During the meetings of bishops conducted over three years, the council emphasized that the church is the whole people of God, not just the hierarchy; that laypeople have a vital role in the church; that there was a need to reach out in a spirit of unity to other Christians and non-Christians; and that there was wisdom in having people participate in the liturgy in their own language rather than in Latin, which was the language of the hierarchy. The ordinary layperson was now encouraged to cultivate their own spiritual authority. We felt energy and hope.

I can still remember how included I felt as the priest celebrating Mass turned around to face the people. He spoke our language and invited us to pray and worship together with him. We were one.

That spirit of collegiality extended to parish organizations, where lay parish councils of women and men were formed to advise the priest on parish affairs. It was a major change for the priest to no longer be the lone hierarchical leader, but now to be a collaborator with the laypeople. Many priests welcomed the new freedom. We older people can still recognize a "Vatican II" priest by his compassion, humility, and down-to-earth demeanor.

But some priests and laypeople found the results of the council to be an abomination. Some ultraconservative clerics didn't want to lose their power. There was a lot of opposition at first. Gradually, however, opposition seemed to lessen.

But, sixty years later, that opposition in the United States is getting louder and louder. This is the result of fundamentalist Catholic clerics having aligned themselves with far-right evangelicals, ultraconservative Catholic laypeople, politicians, and wealthy donors to create a bulwark against Pope Francis and the rest of the church. (It will be interesting to see how our new pope, Leo XIV, will address this disturbing trend.) Once again, extreme conservatives have used Christian nationalism (a melding of church and state in order to retain power) to steer the Catholic Church away from the Christianity of Jesus toward a rigid patriarchal, hierarchical, misogynistic pseudoreligion, where they persecute anyone or anything that doesn't comply with their view of religion and patriotism. Seemingly, these extreme conservatives will do anything to maintain their power.

What the people need from leaders of government and church in difficult times is not a show of force and a return to the dark past, but rather compassion and understanding. Where are our elected officials when we need solutions that benefit the common good rather than deepen partisan divides? Where is the church when we need wise spiritual guidance in traversing the new landscapes of the twenty-first century? According to Mary Jo McConahay, the recent pandemic is an example of this absence of leadership in time of need.

> This capacity to comfort, one might say the responsibility to provide peace and understanding to troubled souls, was particularly violated by bishops and clergy who split from Church counsel and papal example during the pandemic. They inspired fear and division instead, with misinformation. (25)

What we as a nation and a people are enduring now is "institutional grief."

Confronting Our Institutional Grief

Institutional grief is a response to a system or organization that fails to fulfill its promises to protect and care for the people. This phrase popped into my mind recently as I was attending a conference on personal grief at our spirituality center. After I mentioned "institutional grief" as another issue we need to address, a number of women came up to me and affirmed that this is exactly what they are feeling. We have loved our church and our country. But both have failed us, as they have been failing people for centuries. Leaders in the church and government have told us that they are powerful and right, and that we ordinary folk are weak and sinful. This, too, has led to a weakening and loss of our spiritual authority.

Recognizing institutional grief is the first step to reclaiming that spiritual authority. For me, acknowledging the feelings of sadness and shame that I have endured for so long as manifestations of institutional grief has been life-changing. And this has only really happened during the writing of this book. Once I saw how my people, the Saxons, other groups, and women in general have been treated by the patriarchal church and various ruling systems through the centuries, I could viscerally recognize that it wasn't just about me. Whole groups of us have been demeaned, neglected, accused, marginalized, and persecuted by those in power. As we have been forced to accept this treatment, many of us gradually began to believe that maybe we aren't good, maybe we are "less than." I certainly did. I can't count the number of times I cried myself to sleep at night with no consolation in sight.

Walter Brueggemann, a renowned Scripture scholar, has provided some insights into what is happening in our church and culture and what we can do about it. In his book *Reality, Grief, Hope: Three Urgent Prophetic Tasks*, Brueggemann compares the destruction of Jerusalem in 587 BCE with the destruction of our Twin Towers in 2001. He asserts this: "There is no doubt that the destruction of Jerusalem in 587 BCE is the defining historical event in the literature of the Old Testament. That destruction and the dislocation that followed amounted to a huge upheaval of every dimension of Israel's life, including displacement of theological certitude." (1) They thought they were God's chosen ones. Who were they now?

Brueggemann goes on to state that the destruction of 9/11 was the same kind of defining event in the United States. It changed the way we thought about ourselves. "We have been forced to face new waves of vulnerability that we had not before acknowledged." (1) We Americans don't know how to handle vulnerability. After all, we, too, believe that we are God's chosen nation and the shining light to all other nations.

I believe that the COVID pandemic was another one of those defining events for the US. This was, of course, a horror that afflicted the whole world. But again, we had thought we were special, that we were exempt from such disasters. We had to acknowledge that, in fact, we were just one among many countries. The trauma of the pandemic opened up another layer of vulnerability. Unless we can face and accept this vulnerability and see it as a point of growth, we will find ourselves in denial, and denial leads to rage and hopelessness.

Finding a Way to Heal

In each of the events I've just described, institutions, like governments and churches, had to grapple with who they were in this situation and what they were called to do. Unfortunately, instead of bringing people together in compassion and hope, institutional leaders often failed to even acknowledge the reality of the problem or otherwise blamed it on others. This failure was often followed by a return to the old rules and dictates by which powerful white men claimed the ultimate authority in order to keep control of others.

According to Brueggemann, the first task in healing from our institutional grief, like with healing from personal grief, is to move beyond denial and acknowledge our losses. We white Christian Americans too often keep wishing that things would go back to the old days when things were "normal." But the America and the church we thought we knew no longer exist. The United States is no longer number one in the world. Traditional churches are losing influence and membership, as well as being split internally between liberal and conservative alliances.

To heal, we need to accept the truth and openly grieve our losses. We need to publicly speak about our lost hopes, dreams, and beliefs. This speaking openly will probably make us feel very vulnerable and possibly even like we are being traitorous to our country and to our church. However, it is important to voice our grief, because voiced grief eventually leads to letting go. And letting go can open us to new possibilities.

Brueggemann urges us on in this work: "The work of relinquishment . . . must be done! There is no shortcut. . . . [R]elinquishment positions us to receive . . . yet again." (88)

And that's what we need—to receive yet again. We long for a country and a church that are open to the new life all around us. We long for people who will stand up, use their spiritual authority to proclaim the new, the hidden, the possibilities. We need to embrace our goodness and the goodness of others.

Again, I am ranting. "Every day I wake up and have ideas for my book. Unfortunately, it is because every day I am exposed to the craziness that is going on in the United States, its institutions, and even the church. I am just heartbroken! Instead of seeing levelheadedness and a deep desire to do what is best for our country and for our world, I see a playground full of angry two-year-olds willing to obstruct any effort toward the common good until they get what they want. And what they want is surely not the common good! And so many others, though they may not be as immature, do not trust the goodness and strength within themselves and in others. Therefore, they sell their souls to the tyrants and become empty puppets. What a waste!"

Grünthrad nods. "Yes, I've observed the same thing in your country. It reminds me of some of the kings and princes and clerics in my day who acted similarly. I can still feel my frustration and anger with them, and the anxiety and hopelessness of anything getting better."

"And when I wake up," I say, "besides ideas, I feel the burden of speaking out against this madness! That's what my book is about! I'm trying to urge the majority to claim their inner wisdom and speak out for the good. That is what you and your people did. You resisted these grabs for power. You suffered because of it, but you maintained your integrity, at least until centuries moved on and people forgot."

"I hope that doesn't happen to you!" Grünthrad exclaims. "We can't let those powers win! That is why it is so good that you and I are talking. We can support each other."

"Yes, I agree," I say. "This morning, I woke up, having succumbed to fear and loss of hope. What I am trying to achieve seems almost unachievable. My call feels like a terrible burden, and I get terrified. But sharing with you has helped. And I was able to spend a few moments in quiet with my God. And as I listened, God's message broke through my fear and despair. God said, 'I only ask you to do what is yours to do.' This is also what my father Francis of Assisi always said. 'That place is where your passion and focus on the good is most potent and will serve the world the best.' God told me, 'I will be with you, giving you the strength and grace you need to live and proclaim the wisdom of your inner authority.' With God's help, I was able to let go of my ego and my fear, and go off to write."

Grünthrad replies, "I will be helping you from my experience in any way I can."

19

Wake the World

A song released in 2014 by Steven C. Warner, composer and former director of the Notre Dame Folk Choir, captured the words of Pope Francis addressed to women and men religious, urging them to wake up a sleeping world. Titled "Wake the World with Dawning Joy," the song was, and is, an inspirational call not only to women and men religious, but to all people, to recognize goodness in the world and act by claiming our spiritual authority. With lyrics that urge people to work for justice, live in peace, embody human kindness, and love the world, this song is a far cry from the militaristic hymns we sang in the past. This song proclaims joy and goodness.

Isn't this what all of us want? I need to be inspired like this. I'm sure you do also. All the sins I talked about throughout this book, like patriarchy, misogyny, Christian imperialism, racism, persecution of immigrants, continue unabated today. It can be so discouraging! I thought humans might have grown beyond this ugly behavior. But there seems ample evidence that many people are determined to pursue what is patently harmful and even evil.

It can feel worse when seemingly good people turn a blind eye to the evil being perpetuated. They seem or claim to be too busy to be bothered. And then there's another group of people who embrace evil because some guru told them that certain evil acts are okay and even necessary. These people are looking for a savior. So they abandon their own spiritual authority and state with false humility, "I believe it because you say so." "You are so great and I am so little, so I will give up any questioning of this behavior." "I'll do whatever it takes to remain in your good graces."

Following Naked Emperors

This tendency to close our eyes to oppression and injustice and to freely give away our spiritual authority is not a new phenomenon. People have been doing it for centuries. The brilliant story of "The Emperor's New Clothes," written by Hans Christian Andersen in the nineteenth century, provides a good example. Andersen was a Danish author who identified with the poor and the outcast and fought against the oppressive class structure of his time. "The Emperor's New Clothes" could easily have been written in our own time.

It is the story of a vain emperor who was so concerned about himself and how he looked that he paid little attention to his subjects and their needs. Enter two robbers who concocted a scheme to rob the emperor. They promised to make him a set of new clothes, touted as the most magnificent in the empire. He eagerly agreed. But instead of sewing real cloth, they just pretended to sew. It was all an illusion, and through it the robbers raked in a huge amount of money, allegedly spent on the "cloth." Throughout the process, they reassured the emperor that anyone who said they didn't see the cloth was lying, stupid, and not fit for his or her position in the empire. So, when the emperor debuted his clothes during a procession, everyone saw that he was naked, but no one told the truth because they were afraid of reprisal. At one point a small child shouted, "Look, that man is naked!" The child was immediately shushed by his parents, and everyone went back to cheering for the naked emperor.

Do you see the similarity to our time in the US—the lies, the pretense, the pretend admiration for someone who has no substance, the embarrassing servility when people give their dignity away in order to make themselves look good? This pretense is becoming clearer every day. "The Emperor's New Clothes" calls us to be awake to the actual truth of a situation. It urges us to make our own judgments based on facts and evidence, no matter what others think. And it reminds us to speak the truth to power and work against injustice.

Many people throughout the ages have done the same thing as Hans Christian Andersen did, and as Pope Francis did in our time, to challenge others to really wake up to the reality around them. But staying awake implies seeing both the bad and the good.

The Impulse to Look Away

Sometimes I want to close my eyes so I don't see the bad. I did that as a child when I was going to do something risky, like crossing a busy street. I believed that if I didn't look at the cars coming, they wouldn't hurt me. I'm probably alive today because there was little traffic in my small hometown. Today I might not watch the news because it's too terrible. But the trouble with closing our eyes to avoid the bad is that we miss the good that is also happening. The world is such a wonderful, complex place, which makes the chance of seeing exciting new possibilities even greater. I don't want to miss any miracles.

Jesus didn't want us to miss any miracles either. Often he

told his disciples to wake up. For example, in Luke 21, he says, "Be alert at all times." In Mark 14, in the Garden of Gethsemane, Jesus tells the apostles with him to "remain here and keep awake." Here are other examples from the Christian Scriptures:

- "You know what time it is, how it is now the moment for you to wake from sleep. . . . Let us then lay aside the works of darkness and put on the armor of light." (Romans 13:11–12)
- "So then let us not fall asleep as others do, but let us keep awake." (1 Thessalonians 5:6)
- "Devote yourselves to prayer, keeping alert in it with thanksgiving." (Colossians 4:2)

Despite the existence of these verses, there are still so-called Christians who claim to be very religious and yet make fun of being awake, as if it were a bad thing. In the last few decades, we have heard this rhetoric from too many ultraconservative politicians, religious leaders, and rich power-brokers. They often ridicule the word "woke," a term introduced by the African American community to mean being awake to racial prejudice and discrimination. But ultraconservatives change the meaning to urge others to keep their eyes closed to the injustice and abuse that they themselves may perpetrate.

I want to be awake. I want to be aware of the injustices in our nation and around the world. At the same time, I want to see the good. I want to try to act out of my own spiritual authority, not parrot some political or religious figure who is not acting as I would see Jesus doing.

Looking for Goodness

How will we know if we and others are really awake and living the Christian life? The Christian Scriptures tell us the answer: "Beware of false prophets, who come to you in sheep's clothing, but inwardly are ravenous wolves. You will know them by their fruits." (Matthew 7:15–16) Then later in the Scriptures, these fruits are delineated.

As I mentioned earlier, the fruits of the Holy Spirit are love, joy, peace, patience, kindness, goodness, faithfulness, gentleness, and self-control. (Galatians 5:22–23) Many people profess these words, but their actions don't seem to match. If the actions you see from a person or an organization claiming to be Christian reflect blame, polarization, disrespect, and vitriol, then you know that they are only empty vessels spouting meaningless words. On the other hand, if what you hear and see is respect, care for others, and peace-making, then you can recognize them as true followers of Jesus.

Let me focus on one of the fruits of the Spirit—goodness. As I have said before, I have spent my life looking for goodness in myself and others. I believe strongly in this statement recalling the creation of the world from the Hebrew Scriptures, "And God saw that it was good." (Genesis 1) Our sin is in failing to believe this truth, either about ourselves or others. When we emphasize our sinfulness to the extent that the church has done through the years, the search for goodness is difficult but so necessary.

A number of years ago, at a time when I was president of my religious congregation, we introduced to our sisters, affiliates, and partners in mission a process that would help us in this search for goodness. That process is called Appreciative Inquiry. Appreciative Inquiry, formulated by David Cooperrider and his associates at Case Western Reserve University, is the study and exploration of what gives life to human systems when they function at their best. It differs from the traditional approach to organizational change, which focuses on what's wrong or broken. The Appreciative Inquiry approach, in contrast, focuses on what's right in the organization or with the person and builds on it. It asks positive questions and offers prompts like these:

- What is really working well in your life right now? How can you build on it?
- Who has inspired you recently? What was the goodness you witnessed?
- Tell me about a time when you practiced good leadership and empowered others.

In our congregation, we began to ask questions like these in staff gatherings, performance evaluations, meetings, newsletters, and many other venues. The result of our efforts has been an increased unity where people feel good about themselves, and therefore feel called to step forward and share their talent or insight. More people are claiming their own leadership.

Choosing Our Reality

One premise of Appreciative Inquiry that has particularly stood out for me is this: "What you focus on becomes your reality." This means that if I focus on the negative, my reality will consist of anger, frustration, despair, powerlessness, and a lack of creative energy. These reactions are definitely not of the Spirit. But if I focus on the positive, I will be energized, upbeat, hopeful, and creative, and I will naturally attract other good, energetic people.

National Geographic photojournalist and keynote speaker DeWitt Jones embodies this approach. He has created a number of beautiful videos and books with the theme of "Celebrate What's Right with the World." After repeatedly viewing these videos, I always come away inspired and invigorated to find the good all around me. Two quotes from DeWitt's videos stay with me:

- "I learned to reframe obstacles into opportunities by putting a lens of celebration on my camera."
- "Every day we can choose the lens we want to use: Do we want to ask, 'What's the matter with our world?' or do we ask, 'What's right in this situation?'"

We need to live into a new story in order to claim our spiritual authority. Ann Smith, the director of the organization Circle Connections, explains this in an article titled "Circle Connections: The New Story," in Schaaf et al.

> The majority of us on Mother Earth have grown up and lived with the "old story" that . . . separated us, ranking diversity with white over people of color, men over women, straight over gay, people over nature. . . . Living the ways of the "old story" are destroying the planet.
> The New Story brings forth the indigenous ancient stories and a fresh understanding from science that we are One, interconnected and united with God, Creator. The New Story unites us with all creation and, once known in our hearts, opens the floodgates to a greater understanding that we are all loved and magnificent. (55)

This focus on goodness will really wake up the world. Creation is waiting for us to unleash an eruption of good energy. Our focus will change if we truly realize that we are on

Holy Ground. "Holy Ground" implies God's earth. Everyone and every creature around us is full of God. If one believes that within each of us resides a spark of the glory of God, then we can only be true to ourselves if we intentionally share that spark, our spiritual authority, with the world.

Grünthrad approaches a bit uncertainly. "This is difficult for me to say." She hesitates and is quiet for a moment. "You have learned so much from your Scriptures and your religion. You find much truth there." She pauses again. "What about my relationship with my gods? Do you believe that they have truth also? Can you believe that they also inspire me to wake up the world?"

I tell her, "You know I have come a long way from the time when I was a child and young adult when I believed that Catholicism was the only true religion. That kind of thinking leaves out the majority of people in the world."

"Yes, it does," replies Grünthrad.

"I have welcomed stories and insights from many of other faiths," I say. "And getting to know you has deepened my ability to see God and the world differently. You have provided me with an opening into the beauty of Indigenous stories and insights. Thank you."

"I am so relieved! And honored," says Grünthrad. "Thank you. We together are forming the New Story that you talked about in the last chapter. It is so beautiful!"

20

Exposing Christian Imperialism Today

Much of this book has shown how Christian imperialism, the unholy alliance between church and state to maintain power over people, has throughout the centuries caused much suffering among the Saxons and many other peoples around the world. However, Christian imperialism is unfortunately still very much alive today, and causing similar trauma. It is now called Christian nationalism, instead of Christian imperialism because we are a nation now, not a kingdom.

Many people see Christian nationalism, if they recognize it at all, as a theology. But Katherine Stewart, a writer on politics, policy, and religion for various media outlets, challenges that falsehood in her informative and disturbing book *The Power Worshippers: Inside the Dangerous Rise of Religious Nationalism.* She shares the following opinion:

> Christian nationalism is not a religious creed,
> but in my view, a political ideology. It pro-
> motes the myth that the American republic

was founded as a Christian nation. It asserts
that legitimate government rests not on the
reasoned deliberations of the governed, but
on adherence to the doctrines of [a] specific
religious, ethnic, and cultural heritage. (4)

In the US, the doctrines of specific religious, ethnic, and
cultural heritage mean the doctrines of powerful, white, ultraconservative Christian males.

Been there, done that! Isn't this exactly what my ancestors
(and probably yours) suffered at the hands of powerful white
ultraconservative male clerics and rulers in the Middle Ages
and beyond? Men who were determined to claim and retain
"power over" their constituents? This was not the Christianity
of Jesus!

Later in the book, Stewart writes this:

Christian nationalism is also a device for mobi-
lizing (and often manipulating) large segments
of the population and concentrating power in
the hands of the new elite. . . . It actively gen-
erates or exploits culture conflict in order to
improve its grip on its target population. (4)

Remember the culture conflicts that were ramped up by
church and government against pagans, women, other religions, and even scientists in the Middle Ages? Unfortunately,
these same tactics and results are what we are seeing today.

The Church and Christian Nationalism

As I was considering the state of our current world, it occurred
to me that the pandemic was a turning point for me in terms of

how I regarded the unhealthy merging of church and state for power and control over the people. As we all did, I felt physically vulnerable from the threat of disease. But what felt worse to me was that some government officials and Catholic bishops in the United States spread conspiracy theories that told the people that wearing masks and getting vaccinated were part of a plot to control them. These actions kept ordinary people from trusting in God and in the people around them.

The combination of political and religious conspiracy theories reinforcing each other, just like in the Middle Ages with the plague, became very dangerous. Millions of people died, and millions were deprived of the wisdom, help, and consolation that both church and state could have provided.

The fear people experienced was not limited to fear of COVID-19 itself. Let me give you an example. At one point during the pandemic, I took a four-hour car trip through large areas of the state where mask-wearing was considered stupid and even a sign of allying with Satan. I felt fearful each time I had to stop for gas or food, and go into a public building wearing my mask. I wondered, *What will these people do to me, just because my beliefs are different from theirs?*

This is a minor example, nothing at all like the everyday fears of so many Americans. But it is a very real example of the effects of government and religion joining forces to put their people at risk, just so that they can increase their own power. This is Christian nationalism at work.

Using Fear for Power and Control

The US has experienced Christian nationalism many times in its history. Whenever the country goes through a time of chaos and change, movements emerge that try to stop the change by blaming others. An example of this can be seen in the Jim Crow laws in the South after the Civil War. Thomas Hübl explains.

> Despite their legal status as free and rightful citizens, Black Americans living or traveling in the southern states found themselves subject to a powerful set of discriminatory, punitive, and often violent practices enshrined into laws known as Jim Crow. For the better part of a century, these laws enforced racial segregation and resulted in generations of economic, legal, educational, and social inequality. This was possible due to fierce resentments within a powerful white majority, angered by its defeat in the [Civil] War. Using the authority of all available institutions—the law, the church, the schools, and the press—a fierce new regime of white supremacy mobilized to power. (62)

Does this sound familiar? It should. We are seeing this Christian nationalism play out every day.

What Christian nationalists do, essentially, is to instill fear. They stoke that fear for their own purposes—power and control. And they often use violent rhetoric and actual violence, paired with the claim of God's approval, to inflict their will on the people. In US history, the Ku Klux Klan (KKK) was one example of Christian nationalism resorting to violence.

Pairing Jesus and Violence

In our own time, on January 6, 2021, those of us watching national TV saw a similar scenario play out as symbols of violence were paired with Christian imagery for the purpose of stoking actual violence. Andrew L. Seidel, a constitutional attorney and the director of strategic response at the Freedom From Religion Foundation, lists some of the symbols and signs seen on that awful day that proclaimed the Christian nationalist agenda of "spiritual warfare": gallows, nooses, and Confederate flags paired with the cross of Jesus; a flag proclaiming "Born, Raised, and Protected by God, Guns, Guts, and Glory"; and a portrait of Jesus wearing a MAGA hat, to name a few. Seidel continues, "Another haunting image was the militarized man in black carrying a holstered weapon and zip-tie handcuffs . . . photographed as he vaulted the railings in the Senate gallery. . . . Later . . . he commented, 'Jesus saves, and so do guns.'" (Seidel and Tyler, eds., 27–40)

The following verses from Christian Scripture come to mind:

> Then they came and laid their hands on Jesus and arrested him. Suddenly, one of those with Jesus put his hand on his sword, drew it, and struck the slave of the high priest, cutting off his ear. Then Jesus said to him, "Put your sword back in its place; for all who take the sword will perish by the sword." (Matthew 26:50–52)

I want to ask, "You who proclaim to be 'true Christians,' do you not know the real Jesus? Have you not read these words in Christian Scripture?"

Different People, Shared Resentments

All types of people and institutions in the US promote the destructive ideology of Christian nationalism. As noted in the previous quote from Hübl, this ideology emerges out of the fierce resentments held by a powerful white majority angered by defeat: defeat in preventing immigration, defeat in keeping women down, defeat with the reforms of the Second Vatican Council, defeat in elections, and on and on. Mary Jo McConahay explains the situation this way:

> The proponents of white Christian nationalism, after many years of organizing themselves, now include powerful politicians, judges, wealthy donors, Catholic bishops and evangelical ministers, and a whole gaggle of laypeople who have fallen in line with the "gurus." As a far-right group, they want "to implant a nationalist Christian dispensation in the law and culture of the United States, believing that their own moral point of view ought to reign for everybody, throughout the land." (ix)

These various Christian nationalists meet regularly at very expensive conferences where they continue to be indoctrinated by various speakers—not in the principles of Christianity, but in their own power and control agenda. Their common beliefs and goals appear to be a return to the old patriarchal model of family in which the father is in control; keeping women in their place, which is usually in the home; emphasizing that powerful white men are the best hope for a God-blessed nation; and treating immigrants, members of the LGBTQ+ community, people of various non-Christian religions, and others as a threat to our founding as a Christian white nation.

This sounds just like what happened to my Saxon ancestors more than a century ago.

Echoes of the Past

This Christian nationalism of today taps into the trauma of Saxon descendants, whether they consciously recognize it or not. What we are experiencing now is so similar to what happened to Saxons in the eighth century and what happened to numerous groups in the twentieth century at the hands of the Nazis, both in and beyond Germany.

The Nazi Party emerged after Germany's defeat in World War I and the economic problems of the 1920s. Like all Christian nationalist groups, the party appealed to the people most affected by the adverse conditions of the time. In this case, it was the farmers of northwest Germany, the Saxon descendants. The Nazis' message, like the message of all Christian nationalists, emphasized that they had been victimized by the government and the elites, that no one else cared about them, and that they needed to fight back. The Nazis also spread the insidious message that someone needed to be held accountable for all the victimization the farmers felt. In the Germans' case, the Nazis said that someone was the Jews and other non-Aryans.

Martin Goldsmith, an author and American radio personality, writes about the Nazis' rising support in his book *Alex's Wake: The Tragic Voyage of the* St. Louis *to Flee Nazi Germany, and a Grandson's Journey of Love and Remembrance*, which recounts his family's attempt to escape Nazi Germany.

> [T]he Nazi Party had won a small but committed group of followers. In the elections of 1928, the National Socialists attracted 9.8 percent of the vote in the state of Oldenburg [in the former Saxon homelands], earning them a seat on the Oldenburg city council. . . .

> Seven months later, in the elections
> of September 1930, the Nazis polled 27.3
> percent of the Oldenburg state vote. In the
> ensuing months, they began to campaign
> even more heavily in the Northwest, appeal-
> ing directly to the farmers who had been
> among the first in Germany to feel the full
> effects of the Depression. . . . [O]n May 29,
> 1932, 48.4 percent of the voters in the state
> of Oldenburg cast their ballots for the Nazi
> Party. . . . Oldenburg [was] the first state
> in the country to have duly elected Nazi
> leaders. (45)

In that time, Christian nationalism gained a strong foot-hold in rural Germany. Similarly, Christian nationalism today has gained a strong foothold in rural America. US citizens are being told over and over again that they are victims and that the only answer is to rally around Christian nationalist politi-cians, rich businessmen, and hierarchical clerics who will save them and return the country and the church to order and "tra-ditional" values. And they are assured that these figures will save them by any means necessary.

I feel deeply for these rural people because they are my people. I grew up among them, and I know them to be good people. They often don't receive the resources they need from government and church to sustain their livelihoods. As a re-sult, they can get desperate, abandon their own spiritual au-thority, and follow anyone who says he or she can make things better. But too often that claim turns out to be empty rhetoric from people devoid of compassion or any real inclination to help the "little guy." These Christian nationalists are eager to exploit good people in order to gain and preserve power and control.

The Church's Complicity

It is painful to realize it, but at this time there are bishops and others within the Catholic Church who also take this stand. For me, this is very disturbing and frightening. Maybe I shouldn't be surprised, since our church has had a long history of uniting with people in power to scare ordinary people in order to keep them in line. Remember the threats of hell, the witch burnings, the accusations against anyone who had different ideas? All of that is a part of our church that I hate.

And now these Catholic bishops, supported by politicians, wealthy conservatives, and right-wing media, are trying to turn back the clock in the church, just as Pope Pius IX and the First Vatican Council did in the nineteenth century (see chapter 16). Remember that Pope Pius IX grew to profoundly fear the contemporary world. He clamped down on any movement that actually listened to the needs of the people of the modern world. Instead, he called the First Vatican Council that issued the doctrine of papal infallibility, giving the pope ultimate authority and the inability to be wrong in proclaiming certain dogmas concerning faith and morals. He and later popes often excommunicated people who offered alternative theological viewpoints. To protect itself and the power of a white male hierarchy, the official church needed to preserve what it saw as the glorious past in which it had long had complete control.

Within Catholicism today, there is again a strong movement to preserve—and in some cases to return to—the old, the "traditional," which, in this case, means everything that was in place before the Second Vatican Council in the 1960s. This often means opposing what Pope Francis and church councils have said. McConahay points to the Napa Institute, a high-powered ultraconservative Catholic organization of conservative bishops, wealthy donors, and politicians, known for its annual conference teaching attendees how to put into place a new American Catholicism based on "traditional" religion and Christian nationalism.

> The Napa Institute and myriad nonprofit Catholic teaching organizations linked to it offer Catholics what amounts to a parallel magisterium, teaching and sacramental formation that is closer to strict and defensive preconciliar norms than it is to the ecumenical, mercy-centered church led by Francis. . . . Napa's stand is markedly Christian nationalist in its mix of American exceptionalism and the Catholic faith. (61–62)

Like other members of Christian nationalist movements, these prelates, or bishops, are willing to fight anything that threatens white male hierarchy. This fight includes portraying equal rights for women as a threat to the family. Basically, they condemn anything that suggests that laypeople have something to say about what goes on in the church, that women are as valued as men and also possess spiritual authority, that nature is also God's message to the world, or that people of all nationalities and faiths are just as loved by God as they are.

Because these were all values that Pope Francis embraced and preached, these Christian nationalist prelates were vehemently opposed to anything he said or did. Some went to extremes, spouting divisive rhetoric and promoting extreme views. One rogue cleric even proclaimed that Francis should be weighted down by a millstone and thrown into the ocean, thereby resulting in his death. (newsweek.com, October 20, 2023) And this guy claims to be a true Christian. How disgusting!

Mark Markuly, a professor at Seattle University whose area of focus is religion and culture, explains the fear behind the opposition.

> Some were "afraid" that [Pope Francis was] lowering the walls separating the sacred from the profane, going "soft on sin," minimizing the potential consequences of our broken- ness and inadequacies, and inadvertently leading the gullible down the primrose path to perdition. But, Francis [saw] clearly that the Spirit of God does not thrive in cultures of fear, because such communities breed self-righteousness, prejudice, bigotry, and narcissism. (7)

But there is much good news! We can't forget about the green thread of hope, resilience, and new life that is always present with us and within us, and visible to us if we take time to notice.

Holding on to the Green Thread

Much in religious tradition supports and fosters this hope. For example, do you know what the most common phrase is in the Bible? According to various websites, the answer is "Do not be afraid." And guess how many times it appears in its many forms. Anywhere from 120 to 350, depending on who is doing the counting. Specific examples that have spoken to me over the years include Isaiah 41:10, Psalm 46:1–3, and Luke 12:29–32.

Matthew 14:27—Jesus walking on water—is a special fa- vorite of mine. It seems to speak so much to our present circumstances. The disciples are in the boat, overcome by fear and anxiety as a storm rages around them. They are contemplating a watery death. Isn't that how we often feel today in the chaos and fear stirred up by our politicians and other Christian nationalists? I have definitely felt it lately. But Jesus appears, walking on the water, calming their fears. "Take heart," he says, "it is I; do not be afraid."

Carl Koch gives us hope.

> If any lesson or hope for the future can be gained from studying the church's history, it is certainly that the church has always been gifted with the abiding presence of the Holy Spirit. Through times of persecution, internal strife and divisions, and even sinful, misguided mistakes, the church has never been abandoned by God. . . . Even when corruption seemed to tear the church apart, the Spirit of God through people in the church called the church to renewal. (276–277)

Today the Spirit continues to walk with us, urging us not to be afraid to use our spiritual authority to say no to Christian nationalism and to wake up the world.

"I had no idea how pervasive the Christian nationalism agenda has been throughout time," I begin. *"It always seems to stem from men who are afraid of losing their power and afraid of claiming their own true natures, and from women who can't claim their own strength and spiritual authority. How can it keep growing like it does?"*

Grünthrad replies, "I think fear is the answer. My immediate descendants were afraid, and rightfully so. It takes extraordinary courage to stand up to the powers. But let us remember—our family, our descendants and ancestors, did stand up in so many instances. And when they did, things often changed, at least for a while."

"Thank you for reminding me," I say. *"You are right. I just need to keep telling myself the truth. And I need to hear the Spirit of Jesus say, 'Do not be afraid; I am with you.'"*

"I, too, need to reconnect with my gods. They always gave me strength and peace."

I respond, "Let us hang on to the green thread."

21

Saying No to Patriarchy

The first time I had the words to articulate clearly what I had been doing to heal from the shame brought on by patriarchy was when I read Elizabeth A. Johnson's book *She Who Is: The Mystery of God in Feminist Theological Discourse* in the early 1990s. Johnson's articulation of the process of saying no to patriarchy and yes to my good self shook my whole being with the truth I recognized. Please read these words with me.

> There is an experience of lived oppression, interpreted precisely as oppressive and therefore wrong. As the many-faceted dehumanization into which women are cast comes to consciousness . . . a sense of indignation grows. [It] gives rise to a profound and irrevocable *no*. This should not be! The judgment arises: We are worth more than this. Indignation generates the energy for resistance, an act grounded on an equally deep and lasting *yes* to women's flourishing. The search

commences then . . . for new ways of living
that will find what has been lost. (62–63)

These words describe nothing less than a conversion experience. The experience certainly was that for me! I've used
these words whenever I've needed to remind myself to keep
entering into this ongoing conversion.

The positive result of this process is rebirth. This rebirth
is necessary to our healing and to the work God calls us to.
But being reborn in this way is not easy. Many things have im-
proved in society since the various waves of activist women
through the years have brought needed attention to gender
inequality in its various forms. But despite all this hard work,
gender discrimination has had a long and sullied past, and it
has been ingrained in both men and women for generations.
Keep in mind all the examples I gave in part 2 of this book of
the many times and ways a patriarchal society and a hierarchical church joined forces in order to persecute women and keep
them in their place so as to preserve the power and authority
of rich white males. These are the forces we are up against.

Patriarchy Within, Patriarchy Without

When I as a woman feel and hear macro- or micro-aggressions
against me or against women in general, I may immediately feel
undervalued and underestimated. The response is almost auto-
matic. I get angry on the inside but don't often challenge the ag-
gressions out loud. So the feeling festers and turns into shame.
I tell myself, *Maybe I am less qualified and talented than these
men. Maybe there is something basically wrong with me. If I
keep quiet, maybe those in authority just won't notice me. Then
I'll be safe.*

Have you ever had similar inner conversations with

yourself? I would imagine that most women have at one time or another. The result is that women have often been, and continue to be, complicit in patriarchy. Sharon Blackie starkly lays out the underlying reasons for this behavior, which sound a lot like the enforcing arms of patriarchy we've already examined: "Women might have been complicit—we had been well trained for centuries, after all; a little bit of burning at the stake, incarceration in nunneries and lunatic asylums if we didn't do what we were told, and the constant threat of rape and violence: all of them do wonders for compliance." (10)

Such traumas can appear to be inflicted as one-time events, by just one person, independent of any system. But my research has informed me that these acts of aggression and violence do not stand alone. They are part of long-standing efforts by powerful men throughout the ages to keep women in their place. We saw this with patriarchal churches and governments in part 2 of this book. And in fact, there are now organizations and movements in the United States today whose main goal has been to preserve patriarchy.

Mary Jo McConahay's book *Playing God: American Catholic Bishops and the Far Right* lays out the deliberate process, since the Second Vatican Council, of some ultraconservative Catholic bishops and laymen who are trying to turn back the clock, dictate what "true Christianity" should look like and in the process, control women, even women's bodies.

Kristin Kobes Du Mez, professor of history at Calvin University in Grand Rapids, Michigan, in her book *Jesus and John Wayne: How White Evangelicals Corrupted a Faith and Fractured a Nation*, explains a similar long-term process promulgated by ultraconservative American evangelicals and their wealthy donors and supporters to preserve patriarchal family life, in which the father has complete control and the woman serves her husband. According to Kobes Du Mez, "For conservative white evangelicals, the 'good news' of the

Christian Gospel has become inextricably linked to a staunch commitment to patriarchal authority, gender difference, and Christian nationalism, and all of these are intertwined with white racial identity." (6–7)

This one-sided patriarchy has held sway for too long. This is one of the reasons I felt I needed to write this book about reclaiming our spiritual authority. I want to become more and more aware of patriarchy whenever and wherever it raises its ugly head, and I want to speak up personally and collectively in an authoritative way against all discrimination.

Can you imagine the power we could wield as women if we bonded together and worked for the common good?

Women Wielding Power

We do not have to only imagine it. We can look around us to see other women doing this work. One significant example of this type of group power emerged in 2009, when the Vatican informed the Leadership Conference of Women Religious (LCWR), made up of the leaders of 66 percent of women's Catholic religious communities in the US, that it had grave concerns about the leadership and orthodoxy of the conference. (For a more complete explanation of the situation, see the excellent book *However Long the Night: Making Meaning in a Time of Crisis*, edited by Immaculate Heart of Mary Sister Annmarie Sanders.) This pronouncement provoked shock, anger, and sadness among LCWR members and their many supporters around the country. People wanted the leaders to fight back publicly, to use their power in a dominating and accusatory way. But the leaders and members of LCWR chose to engage in a process of using power in a way that sought healing rather than division.

A brief overview of the process highlights the elements important in using power in a way that brings people together.

First of all, the LCWR leadership, members, and their member congregations entered into a process of contemplative prayer and discernment that led to a deep grounding in God. They reviewed and affirmed the LCWR mission, which provided them with clarity. Also, from the beginning and throughout the process, the group offered opportunities for people to surface, express, and process their strong emotions in a safe environment.

These actions freed them up to engage in open and respectful dialogue with Vatican representatives. LCWR leaders committed themselves to speaking truth, listening deeply, and opening themselves to be transformed while simultaneously retaining the integrity of the organization. The leadership vowed to faithfully continue the dialogue for as long as it took. In the end, six years later, both sides had attained deeper respect for each other.

Practicing Shared Power

This process has become a model for others in negotiating polarization, conflict, and misunderstanding with integrity and communion intact. Shared power happens when qualities like collaboration, compassion, intuition, emotional intelligence, relationality, and seeing the world as connected, are used to create new models of nonpatriarchal leadership.

This was not an entirely new thought. Already by the fourteenth century, Julian of Norwich (introduced in chapter 13) had laid out a theology and philosophy that challenged patriarchy, as Matthew Fox explains in *Julian of Norwich: Wisdom in a Time of Pandemic—and Beyond*.

> Julian takes on the privilege and dangers of
> patriarchy by deconstructing it. Instead of
> a punitive Father God, she presents us with

a loving, Mother God. Instead of exalting
survival for the few, she declares a democracy
of justice and caring. Instead of a dualism of
body vs. soul, masculine vs. feminine, human
vs. nature, she proclaims unity. Instead of fear,
trust. Instead of leading with the reptilian
brain, she thinks with the mammal, cooper-
ative brain. Instead of raping and plundering
Mother Earth, she honors the divine in nature
and the "web of creation" that Hildegard
wrote about. (124)

Unfortunately, there are still people who rail against
anything that threatens to take away patriarchal power. For
example, did you know that there is an "E-*man*-gelization"
movement afoot? There are websites, podcasts, speeches,
books, and articles devoted to arguing that the church has become too "feminized," that masculinity is in crisis. Oh, really?

Those making this claim think that men (and therefore
the church) should be more militaristic and fight back. After
all, they argue, men are the strong ones who can defend the
faith and conquer the enemies of the faith. These emangelists
believe the church should appeal to men in this manner. And,
absurdly, adherents within the Catholic Church propose that
one small way to accomplish this would be to mandate that,
once again, as it used to be, only boys can be altar servers;
that way, they say, the boys won't be intimidated by girls and
can learn to be real men. Believe me, I'm not making this
stuff up.

Brené Brown, whom I mentioned as one of the foremost
experts on shame, asserts that, despite this movement's
claims, most men would like to be more balanced rather than
being always expected to hide their feelings, to be strong, to be
aggressive, to never admit they're wrong. They may be able to

maintain this image on the outside, but underneath, they fear being seen as weak. They have been taught this approach all their lives. Remember how my Saxon ancestors were taught the same thing—how the men were forced to become perpetual warriors, never allowed to enjoy ordinary peace and harmony?

If there is a crisis of masculinity in our world, it is not a weakening of masculinity; rather, it is a crisis of "toxic masculinity," as described by Richard Rohr, in which some men think they have to retain control and power because they are too afraid of embracing other sides of themselves, like compassion, vulnerability, mercy, respect, cooperation—you know, kind of like Jesus would do. The really strong men that I know are able to love, extend mercy, be vulnerable, and work with others to make the world a better place. We need more of these truly good men.

Things have to change. Otherwise, we as a country will continue to be stuck in the dysfunction that we are now experiencing. The journalist Mary Ann Sieghart quotes former Irish President Mary McAleese from her interview with her.

> If men don't take women . . . seriously, we end
> up with this world that flies on one wing . . .
> It can't get elevation; it can't get direction; it
> flaps about rather sadly. And that's our world,
> flapping about rather sadly because of the
> refusal to use the elevation and the direction
> and the confidence that comes from flying on
> two wings.
>
> And the sad thing is that very often this
> male wing seems to think it has to spend a lot
> of effort keeping the other wing down. And
> that's wasted effort, it's wasted lives. . . . [We]
> have to understand that when women flourish

and their talents and their creativity flourish,
then the world flourishes and men flourish.
We all flourish. (308)

In a world searching for hope, we need only look around us to find it. We have everything and everyone we need to bring about healing and wholeness, if only we are willing to embrace everyone and their contributions in order to get there.

"Your words have reminded me of how my male descendants became even more warlike than they had been once they were told that Jesus was a conquering savior and they needed to be his army, subduing anyone who didn't agree with them," muses Grünthrad. "This attitude then carried over to their families. They became harsher at home, even sometimes beating their wives. And their wives became silent because they feared for their lives. What made it even worse was that the church told them that a good wife never opposes her husband, and she must be submissive." Grünthrad looks very sad as she remembers. "But what you have told me is that your God and this Jesus would never have wanted this. They preached love, not hate."

"The tragedy is that this patriarchal nonsense is still happening," I say. "Now, more than ever, we need to stand up and do something about it. We are more knowledgeable and aware that there are many people who think the same way."

Grünthrad adds, "And now you have more and faster ways to spread the word."

"Yes, I've seen people across the globe mobilize around revolutions through social media."

"Like you said, let the revolution begin!" Grünthrad exclaims.

22

Welcoming the "Other"

Are we (you and I) willing and able to embrace everyone, men and women, people of other nationalities, ages, sexual orientations, social classes, political orientations, and nonhuman life such as that found in nature—that is, everyone else both like us and unlike us? All of these beings are the source of a vibrant, interesting, growthful, and productive future. But somehow, when we are invited or challenged to do this, many of us get nervous and afraid. We feel that we need to protect ourselves and our own, that if we open ourselves to others, we will lose ourselves. Thomas Hübl elaborates on the depth and scope of this fear.

> Millennia have passed since safety was the predominant daily concern of most humans, but when layers of cultural trauma become activated, large portions of even advanced societies return to the primary drive of this earlier stage of evolution. From within it, we view the stranger as deadly or undeserving; the

> foreigner as alien. Strong feelings of caution
> and a desire for distance must be processed
> before we can come into relation with individ-
> uals or groups that are unknown to us. (94)

I can identify with this fear, both personally and intergen-
erationally. Remember how my Saxon ancestors learned to
"barricade" themselves in homogeneous communities, both in
the German lands and in the United States? I would imagine
that your history includes similar stories.

As I said earlier, I grew up in a very homogeneous small
town—everyone was white, Catholic, German, and involved in
farming. We were proud of our community. But this type of en-
clave usually has a hard time welcoming diversity. Admittedly,
we didn't have many opportunities to do so.

However, that time of relative contentment has changed
a lot since I was a child. Most rural states nationwide have
experienced declines in population, the number of younger
families, the economy, access to vital services like health
care, quality education, internet, and on and on. Rural people
often feel alone, like nobody understands what they are going
through. And I don't blame them.

But again, as in the Middle Ages and throughout history,
rather than uniting as a people and welcoming others of various colors, creeds, talents, dreams, and viewpoints, too often
we seem to embrace *blame*, almost as if it were a snuggle toy.
"Everything will be all right if we just hang on to blame."

As Thomas Hübl proclaimed in the passage above, we
want to blame the "other." Well, that hasn't worked in the past,
and it won't work now. *Blame* simply destroys communities
and doesn't build anything.

Recently I found a very timely book titled *White Rural
Rage*, written by Tom Schaller and Paul Waldman, who both
have roots in rural America. They lay out the hardships of

rural America and suggest ways for residents to claim their strengths and work together with other rural Americans—white, Black, Hispanic, Native American, Asian—to reclaim their power.

They quote Douglas Burns, a blogger and columnist for the rural *Carroll Times Herald* in western Iowa. (I particularly noticed this quote because my Saxon ancestors had moved to Carroll County in the later decades of the nineteenth century, once the good land ran out near New Vienna, my hometown.) In 2022, Burns wrote this in an article titled "As Rural Americans We Must See Ourselves as Part of the Nation's Diversity": "We rural Americans need to focus on finding allies in other demographics who are similarly left out of the modern American economy and higher education and top levels of the judiciary—and yes, even my profession, journalism, where rural voices can be absent or hard to find in key power centers." (225)

I hope that we Saxon descendants can let go of our fear and blame and open ourselves to welcoming diversity and the resulting opportunities. Because the truth is this: Although we may fear the "other," actually there *is* no "other" to be afraid of. We are one. Our call is to respect and listen to each other and build relationships. This work is not easy. But once you forge a relationship with a person or a group, they are no longer "the other" because you see them and know them at a deeper level. You are no longer afraid.

Partnering with the "Other"

In my life, I have been privileged to be a part of some awesome examples of the power of building relationships with those I used to regard as "other." One example that tugs deeply on my heart involves our country's relationship with Native Americans.

Growing up, I didn't know any native people. But my dad recalled that his father talked about having small groups of "Indians" ask permission to cross what he called "our" land, permission that he gave them. Only now does it occur to me to ask, "Why did they need permission to cross the land? Wasn't it theirs or, at least, wasn't it everyone's land?" But back then, all I knew was what church and society had taught us, which was that these "Indians" were pagans and enemies, people who needed to be defeated and converted.

Later, though, after I had entered religious life, I had opportunities to expand my horizons. In the 1970s, a small group of sisters and I visited the Rosebud reservation of Sioux in South Dakota for a couple of weeks. Our purpose was simply to get to know the people there and see if we could help them. I remember feeling like we shouldn't be there, recognizing that we weren't any kind of saviors, understanding that these people were brave, resilient, and capable of controlling their own lives.

During our stay, our small group visited Wounded Knee, site of the historic battle, which at that time in the 1970s had again become a powder keg in the fight for Indigenous rights. I was deeply moved by the ongoing suffering and abuse endured by the Native Americans and their strength to resist. Even though I didn't have contact again with this people for a long time, I continued to feel an inner sense of care and concern for them.

Another experience appeared more recently when our congregation of sisters began to realize that our organization had been complicit in horrible colonizing efforts against the Bad River band of Ojibwe in northern Wisconsin. FSPA had staffed an Indian boarding school there from 1883 to 1969. At the time, it was one of almost five hundred such schools in the United States, most of them run by the government but a significant number staffed by Catholic religious orders.

Our congregation's intention of helping the Indigenous

peoples to know Jesus and to provide the education we thought they needed had seemed good at the time. Since then, we have learned from the long-term effects on the people just how wrong we were. We had seen the children as "other" and felt that they should adapt to white Christian culture. That entailed cutting their hair, dressing them in "white man's clothes," making them speak English, and teaching them our religion.

FSPA now acknowledges with deep sorrow the harm we caused to the children of the tribe and to their families by efforts to destroy their culture, language, religion, and very existence. Amanda Skenandore, in her fictional book *Between Earth and Sky*, powerfully describes the internal harm the Indian boarding schools caused.

> Have you ever pulled back the husk of a corn and found that the inside is empty, all the kernels have been eaten away by a worm or field mouse and only the cob is left? You can feel it when you hold it—it's lighter than the other ears, has trouble holding its shape. . . . That's what we're like, those of us returned from Stover or Carlisle or Haskell [government-run native boarding schools]. Peel back the husk and we're empty, hollowed out. The Indian in us is eaten away. (194)

With God's grace, our congregation began to take responsibility for our actions. Writers and activists Enns and Myers quote Indigenous filmmaker Nikki Sanchez in reminding us, "This history is not your fault, but it is absolutely your responsibility." (12) In 2018, FSPA set a congregational direction to challenge our white privilege and work toward equity and inclusion of all.

In 2020, our FSPA congregation and our partners in mission

formed a Truth and Healing Team to take the lead and help us listen to the painful and tragic experiences of Indigenous communities. We also became members of the National Native American Boarding School Healing Coalition and helped sponsor a White Privilege Symposium in La Crosse in 2021.

Next, we began to build relationships with local members of both the Bad River band of Ojibwe in northern Wisconsin, whose children had attended our boarding school, and the Ho-Chunk Nation, since FSPA's Saint Rose Convent in La Crosse occupies the unceded ancestral and traditional land of the Ho-Chunk. Together we have listened to each other to build trust. We have engaged in common activities. Recently, our former FSPA president appeared briefly in the powerful film *Bad River*, released in 2024, which chronicles the ongoing trauma of the Bad River band of Ojibwe and their deep resilience that continues to this day. In the film, she publicly acknowledged FSPA's complicity in the harm done to native children and our part in the cultural genocide of Indigenous people. The relationship of FSPA members with tribe members is in the beginning stages, and, although we can never undo the past, we are committed to show up, listen deeply, demonstrate our respect, learn from each other, and share with vulnerability.

Another big step forward for the relationship between the US Catholic Church and Indigenous people occurred in June 2024, when the United States Conference of Catholic Bishops formally apologized for its role in the Indian boarding schools. The apology got mixed reviews from the native people, but it is a move toward healing.

Our Mother as Other

Another example of the need for relationship building with the "other" is found in our relationship with Mother Earth. In earlier chapters, we talked about how nature was for centuries viewed in a very negative light by the church and other ruling powers. The natural world was then, and still is, seen by many as the property of humans, to be dealt with in any way needed to keep it under control.

This attitude and belief have led to some devastating consequences in our own time: planetary warming, more unprecedented destructive weather events, melting of the glaciers, endangered species of animals, droughts, wildfires, destruction of the ozone layer, and on and on. And all this is the result of our collective trauma and our need to control. Anthony M. Stevens-Arroyo notes the following:

> Faced with the exploitation and destruction of the planet being conducted by unfettered enterprise, ecological preservation has become a moral issue for civilization. Until now, "going green" has generally been cast as a stylish fad of elites whose concern for endangered species somehow stands in the way of business, jobs, and capitalism. It would not be difficult to find disdainful references from noise radio about "the tree huggers." But what if those "tree huggers" presented themselves instead as "God-lovers"? (10–11)

Saint Francis is one of those "God-lovers." He treated all parts of creation as brothers and sisters. Another one of those "God-lovers" was Pope Francis. From early on in his papacy, he made known the importance of caring for the environment. In 2015, Pope Francis wrote his second encyclical, or letter to the people, entitled *Laudato Si: On Care for Our Common Home.* In it, he promotes an "integral ecology," a holistic approach that connects humans and the environment. The way to heal the environment is to address human and societal problems like poverty, economic inequity, and forced migration. All of these are caused by human greed and by people's attempts to control nature.

The Other "Others"

When governments, churches, or individuals become afraid of losing power and control, there is no limit to the "others" that we may reject or even persecute. These people may include immigrants, people of other non-Christian religions or political parties, the LGBTQ+ community, the poor, and more. We in effect dehumanize them so that we can claim our number one status.

The Other, Myself

Someone else we often treat as "other" is ourselves. Unfortunately, many of us do not know our real selves. We live out of a "victim" mentality ingrained in us centuries ago by patriarchal rulers and passed down to us through intergenerational trauma. We can't see ourselves as good and powerful beings, created by God to make a difference in the world by owning our spiritual authority. Rather, we too often see ourselves as victims and look elsewhere for someone to save us. In this way, we deny our real selves.

A Community of Others

So many others! But what if all we "others" would unite for the common good of the world? It's possible. But first, we really need to experience one another as brothers and sisters. "Encuentro" is a Spanish word popularized by Pope Francis throughout his papacy in writings and speeches. It means a gathering or meeting with others, especially with those outside our usual groups and people who are on the margins, to engage with them through listening and fostering dialogue. If we were to do this, we might soon see that we all are one.

Pope Francis, when he addressed the US Congress in 2019, changed the frame of reference on the immigration issue when he used the word "neighbors" for people we often consider "other" and urged us not to turn our backs on them. An ideal image of neighbors is that they are people whom we don't just live next to, but whom we actually know. But no one starts out knowing their neighbors. Even our closest neighbors started out as strangers—or as the other.

This is no more true than it is in the case of our immigrant neighbors, whose cultures or language may be new and unfamiliar to us. Immigrants have moved next door to many of us, as immigrants always have, in countless places throughout the world. These people desire a better life and want to be good neighbors to us. This can be the case not just proximally but also relationally. Let us all give them a chance.

Sister of St. Joseph Pat Kozak, a process facilitator and consultant for religious congregations, worded this idea so beautifully in an article in *Give Us This Day*. (September 29, 2024)

> Our mindsets and expectations often do
> not see the possible colleagues and partners
> there before our eyes. When we look for who
> belongs, we often look for people who speak
> like us, who think and look like us. Perhaps if
> we simply look for partners in human kind-
> ness, for people of goodwill, we might dis-
> cover it is we who are being welcomed into

an incredible, beloved community already
around us.

To welcome others—as neighbors, as friends, as brothers
and sisters—we need to unearth and dismantle the racism
that is a big part of our nation. This work certainly isn't easy,
as I learned recently when I attended the viewing of the film
Deconstructing Karen and the discussion that followed. The
documentary is about two women of color, Regina Jackson and
Saira Rao, who have brought white women together to engage
in deep conversations about racism in the United States and
our part in it.

During the discussion, the people leading it asked, "Who
in this room is a racist?" No one raised her hand. Next, the
leaders asked, "Who in this room would choose to be a Black
woman or woman of color?" Again, no one raised her hand.
Then the leaders replied, "And that itself shows your racism."
Wow! (You can read more about their process in *White Women:
Everything You Already Know About Your Own Racism and
How to Do Better.*)

This discussion was very uncomfortable for me because
my name is Karen, which has recently become a stereotype or
meme for a middle-class white woman who feels entitled to
weaponize her white privilege against Blacks and other people of color. But mostly my discomfort stemmed from having
to confront my own racism, as did everyone else in the room.
I was reminded of how I had been challenged by the Dalai
Lama's words cited at the beginning of this writing journey:
"The world will be saved by the Western [white] woman." Now
I know that we will do this by confronting our own racism.
Facing the daunting task of dismantling my racism is difficult,
and I feel anxious, unsure, and afraid. But I am committed to
walk this journey.

Resmaa Menaken, a licensed counselor and expert in

conflict and violence, states the following in his groundbreaking book *My Grandmother's Hands*:

> When European settlers first came to this
> country centuries ago, they brought a mil-
> lennium of intergenerational and historical
> trauma with them, stored in the cells of their
> bodies. Today, this trauma continues to live
> on in the bodies of most Americans. . . . [But]
> we are at a reckoning. . . . For centuries, it was
> possible for white Americans to accept the
> white-body supremacy without questioning
> it; to enjoy its privileges and to take them
> for granted; and to ignore or deny the ways
> in which white-body supremacy routinely
> harmed dark bodies. Those days are now over.
> (294, 296)

Each of us needs to do our own work. We white people
must heal ourselves, as must Black and other people of color.
Once we have achieved this healing, then we can welcome
each other's gifts and work together to heal the world.

Grünthrad begins, "It is difficult for me to even remember what being welcomed feels like. For so, so very long, we Saxons were rejected and persecuted by everyone. We were seen as 'other' because we were pagans or because we loved Mother Earth or because we were too independent or because we were not loyal enough. People were afraid of us, and therefore lashed out at us. It has been so painful; that is, until you showed up, and really wanted to talk to me. I am so grateful!" She pauses, seemingly to gather her thoughts. "But to be honest, I have probably been just as guilty of rejecting the 'other.'"

"I likely have done the same thing," I reply. "Remember, I was raised in an insular environment where we didn't really know anyone outside of our religious and cultural group. Plus, as a white woman in the US, I have lived a privileged life. I felt compassion for the suffering of other groups who were discriminated against. But it never went deep enough to really move me to do much." I spend a bit of time thinking. "But now that I've somewhat awakened, I need to face the fact that I am racist. Guilt and shame assault me. But those feelings don't help. I need to stand up and do something. I have begun the process of healing and change with the help of some wonderful guides, including you. Your sharing of your trauma has helped me to begin to understand."

Grünthrad says, "I am happy for you. May you be blessed by your God. And let us continue to share. That will help both of us."

23

Reclaiming Our
Spiritual Authority

Now I have come to a milestone on my journey to claim my spiritual authority. Hopefully, as you have read these words, you also have begun the work of claiming yours. I have gained strength through communing with Grünthrad, from sitting in silence and hearing her stories of trauma and resilience. I have felt supported and inspired by the stories of people who, throughout the centuries, challenged hierarchical and patriarchal authorities when they just knew that what they were being told was wrong. And they didn't only challenge the authorities. They promoted a way forward that emphasized the life-giving message of Jesus and the Spirit.

Lessons from the Saxons

Let me summarize a bit of the wisdom I have learned from my ancestors, the Old Saxons. First of all, the Saxons saw no divide between spirituality and nature. They were Indigenous people, meaning they were people of the land. They cared about their land, felt at home there, and wanted to protect it. They worshipped in nature, because they innately realized that the natural world is where their gods were to be found. The Saxons valued the sun, the moon, the land, trees, and water, and they welcomed the crops their gods bestowed upon them. They followed the natural rhythms of time and the seasons. They were also in tune with their bodies and saw them as natural.

In contrast, people today have been so focused on intellectual concepts and artificial constructs that we have lost sight of the wisdom of nature and the natural processes. Too often we have demeaned our bodies and creation as a whole. Why do we think we are so bad and sinful when everything about us is amazing? God created us, after all; we are sparks of the Divine. If we spend more time communing with nature, we will want to preserve it and come to know God at a much deeper level.

A second piece of wisdom from my ancestors, the Old Saxons, is their belief that all members of the community were important, and each had something to contribute to the well-being and survival of the tribe. The Saxons were a unique group in that they had no king; no one person was above the others. They trusted in the wisdom of their gods to call forth various leaders at various times. And in this way, power did not reside permanently in one man.

Third, the Saxons loved their gods, who were very present to them. These gods were part of everyday life; everything revolved around them. Consequently, the Saxons were focused on the present, not on a future in a heaven far away. Before Charlemagne, they never focused on sin or saw themselves as bad. Their actions were influenced by the needs of the community—whatever would sustain a good life for everyone. Women were very much a part of this endeavor. Their gifts of understanding the movements of the natural world, bringing healing to clan members, and generally sustaining life made them extremely valuable. Men and women prayed to male and female gods.

Finally, I have learned that the Saxons were a strong, assertive, and energetic people willing to pursue a better life. Even after they were conquered and had to forget their culture, it was often the Saxon survivors and descendants who throughout history pushed for change and reform. They gathered with others to create reform movements. Now that I know all this, when I am feeling beaten down, I can remember this characteristic of my ancestors, which gives me renewed strength and purpose.

Following in the Footsteps of the Saxons

As I have worked on my book, I have come to realize that claiming these gifts of my Saxon ancestors might help all of us to move beyond the intergenerational trauma that we survivors—and we are all survivors—have allowed to control us for too long. We no longer need to live as slaves to shame or anger or to a victim mentality. We can claim our resilience, strength, and goodness. We don't need someone else to save us. We already are surrounded by our neighbors (new and old) who will walk with us, and we together can change the world.

At this point, you may be wondering if I have remained in the Catholic Church and, if so, why. I have not hesitated to bring forward critiques of the church. But also remember that I have celebrated the church and its members when it has followed the green thread of the Holy Spirit, proclaiming love and goodness in the world.

The Catholic Church is my heritage. I love many things about my church, including its emphasis on beauty, art, and music. I cherish the legacy of spiritual direction down through the ages. Even though I don't always agree with the theology of certain scholars, I value that we have a long history of theological and spiritual writings. I am so grateful that the Catholic Church has many organizations that provide aid for the poor, the migrant, all those in need. I love sitting in church in the quiet and taking in the beautiful mystery of God. And I value religious life, which has helped make me who I am.

So, yes, I have chosen to remain in the Catholic Church. But I will continue to critique and challenge the church when my spiritual authority indicates to me that I must.

Remember Dorothee Sölle's "hermeneutics" of suspicion and hunger, which I introduced in chapter 10? At this point on our journey, I think we are ready to be vulnerable enough to use the "hermeneutic of hunger." We have considered with suspicion. Now it is time to ask the question: What is it that will fill us up? What is it that we deeply desire, both for Christianity and for the United States?

Your answers must come from you. As for me? One thing I hunger for is a Catholic Christian Church that emphasizes the inspiration and power of the Holy Spirit. In the past, the church tended to intellectualize faith, making a belief in doctrines—especially those that concern God the Father and God the Son—and not the embodied experience of living out faith in love the most important indication of being a true Catholic. Many Catholics were quite content with this intellectualized and prescribed religion, and still are. They want to know exactly what is expected of them in order to get to heaven, and then they feel justified in judging others for *not* living out a "correct" faith.

The path forward for a viable theology and spirituality for the twenty-first century is to focus more on an experiential, down-to-earth, enlivening, inclusive, and participatory church. Good news! Pope Francis already called for this focus in Catholic theology. He urged a Catholic theology and spirituality that is less abstract and prescriptive and more pastoral, as well as rooted in reflection on the concrete situations in which people find themselves, in a variety of cultures and contexts. This is the same thing Pope John XXIII wanted in calling the Second Vatican Council in the 1960s. He envisioned a church that would adapt to the modern world of the 1960s, just like we need to adapt to our world today.

To initiate this new theological view, Pope Francis called for a global synodal process of listening to the entire church, not just episcopal authorities, regarding issues that are affecting everyone. Over a three-year period, Catholics in every diocese around the world were invited to interact with each other, discuss with vulnerability, and tell stories of their own experiences in order to get a fuller picture of what Catholicism is at this time in history.

The German bishops (with whom I imagine I share some of my Saxon ancestors) began a similar process in 2019, even before Pope Francis's invitation. These German bishops were alarmed by the number of Catholics in their dioceses who were leaving the church after the clergy sex-abuse scandal. They realized that they needed to listen to the people. So together they gathered 230 clergy and laypeople to address four topics: power in the church, relationships and sexuality, priestly ministry and celibacy, and women in ministries and offices in the church.

Colleen Dulle, an associate editor at *America Magazine* and cohost of the *Inside the Vatican* podcast, noted this about the gathering: "[A] look at the German synodal path finds a church that sees its deep woundedness and that is willing to work together despite differences of opinion to address the root problems of the abuse crisis so that it can become credible." (5) This is the kind of church for which I hunger—vulnerable, collegial, recognizing the worth of all peoples.

But this openness and collegiality of the church's synodal process has frightened some people in the church and led to critique. They want to close the windows again and adopt a bunker mentality, the very thing that the Second Vatican Council sought to dismantle. They don't seem to recognize the green thread of the Spirit of God that is among us, leading us forward at this moment, just as the Spirit has been doing all through history.

For what else do I hunger? I hunger for a church and society that are less focused on sin, blame, and punishment and more focused on gratitude, grace, compassion, building relationships, embracing goodness, and welcoming all. The question should not be what is *wrong* with someone, but what is *right* and *good* about them. I have written about this hunger throughout this book.

I also hunger for a church in which social justice is again embraced as an important element of being Catholic. This aspect of the church seems to have been overlooked at times. But, in 1891, Pope Leo XIII issued an encyclical entitled *Rerum Novarum: On Capital and Labor* in response to the harmful effects of the Industrial Revolution. According to Richard P. McBrien, author of *Catholicism* and former professor of theology at Notre Dame, this was the first time that the church issued "a clearly discernible body of official teachings on the social order, in its economic and political dimensions." (912)

In his book, McBrien goes on to describe the functioning of Catholic social teaching. Catholic social teaching has continued to develop with each new political or economic issue facing the human community, from nuclear warfare, to peace, to new developments in technology, to ecological devastation, and many others. Primary tenets of all these teachings are the dignity of the human person; the prioritization of needs of the poor and vulnerable; the dignity of work and the rights of workers; the common good; and care for God's creation. (912–916)

I hunger for a church and culture that will truly embrace

Mother Earth. She has been waiting a long time for this. Because of my Saxon ancestors and their worship of the Divine in nature, and thanks to my own background of being raised on a farm, I have always felt more connected to God in nature than in buildings. I hope that before it is too late, we all can realize the importance of recognizing the revelation of God that comes to us through all of the cosmos, not just in texts and buildings. Maybe my Saxon kinfolk, who have felt a deep affinity for the earth, can be instrumental in spreading the word.

Part of embracing Mother Earth is loving our bodies. Somehow, we as Christians have been led to believe that we need to distrust our bodies and even go so far as hating them. The patriarchal church has instilled this distrust in many ways throughout the centuries, from declaring women witches for employing their knowledge of life processes in healing to treating any sexual sin as an offense almost worse than murder. Our bodies are good. If we can acknowledge this fact, we will be able to also see other bodies as gifts of the Divine.

Our Desires, Our Spiritual Authority

If all of the above is what I hunger for and deeply desire in Catholic Christianity and in the United States, then claiming my desires as God's desires is the act of claiming my spiritual authority. Speaking that truth is my call in the world. We are all called to be prophets, because speaking the truth is what prophets do. I love the following story about Eldad and Medad in the Hebrew Scriptures:

> Then the Lord came down in the cloud and
> spoke to him [Moses], and took some of
> the spirit that was on him and put it on the
> seventy elders; and when the spirit rested

upon them, they prophesied. . . . Two men
remained in the camp, one named Eldad, and
the other named Medad, and the spirit rested
on them [and they prophesied]. . . . Joshua
. . . the assistant of Moses, . . . said, "My Lord
Moses, stop them!" But Moses said to him,
"Are you jealous for my sake? Would that all
the Lord's people were prophets, and that the
Lord would put his spirit in them!" (Numbers
11:25–29)

I love the line "Would that all the Lord's people were
prophets." That is our call.

But claiming the title of prophet is often difficult.
Sometimes we especially hesitate when reform is called for
within our own church or country. We may feel like traitors if
we speak out. Cardinal Robert McElroy of the archdiocese of
Washington, DC, reflects on this:

Our love for the faith community that is our
home and treasure leads us at times to deny
or hide harsh defects in the Catholic communion. We feel compelled to present and
defend a counterfeit church, devoid of error
and sin. . . . A synodal church genuinely seeks
to discern its woundedness and embrace
reform. (9)

One example of a modern-day prophet who challenged
her own church is a woman from my own FSPA community,
Sister Thea Bowman. In the 1970s and 1980s, Sister Thea be-
came a national leader and advocate for Black Catholics. As a
Black woman, she recognized how marginalized the Catholic
Church had often kept her people.

Through her passionate speaking, singing, and delightful humor, Sister Thea became a prophetic witness against racism in the church. She wasn't afraid of making people feel uncomfortable. She even managed to get the US Catholic bishops at their semiannual meeting to stand together and sing "We Shall Overcome." Now that is discomfort! Though she wasn't always accepted, Sister Thea used her voice to make a powerful difference. Mike Wallace, who interviewed Sister Thea for CBS *60 Minutes* in 1987, remarked in the foreword of the book *Sister Thea Bowman, Shooting Star: Selected Writings and Speeches*, "I don't remember when I've been more moved, more enchanted by a person whom I've profiled, than Sister Thea Bowman." Today she is being considered for sainthood because she found good in the world and proclaimed it to the rooftops.

Sister of Mercy Theresa Kane was another prophet who spoke truth to power. She was one of the founding mothers of the women's ordination movement in the Catholic Church and was passionate about advocating for women priests. In 1979, she was the president of the Leadership Conference of Women Religious when Pope John Paul II made his first papal visit to the US.

In front of the large audience at the Basilica of the National Shrine of the Immaculate Conception in Washington, DC, she said this to the pope: "The church, in its struggle to be faithful to its call for reverence and dignity for all persons, must respond by providing the possibility of women as persons being included in all ministries of our church." Kane went on to say, "Anything less . . . is not only wrong—it is a scandal to our church and our world." (This quote was reported by Jason DeRose, on National Public Radio's *Weekend Edition*, August 31, 2024, on the event of her death.)

Like Sister Thea Bowman, Sister Theresa felt she had to share what her inner voice was telling her. She had to use her spiritual authority. Once we have claimed our inner voice, the universe calls us to share it more widely. It calls us to unite with others (ancestors, partners in mission, neighbors, the next generations) to work together for justice.

As Elizabeth A. Johnson writes in her groundbreaking *Friends of God and Prophets*, the Holy Spirit (also known as Holy Wisdom) is among us always, urging us to be the green threads weaving together a hopeful future.

> Down through the centuries, as Holy Wisdom
> graces person after person in land after land,
> situation after situation, they form together
> a grand company of the friends of God and
> prophets; a wisdom community of holy people
> praising God, loving each other, and struggling
> for justice and peace in this world; a company
> that stretches backward and forward in time
> and encircles the globe in space. (41)

Now that I have finished writing this book, I feel different from three years ago. I am less afraid of being wrong and more willing to be a leader, helping others to claim their own goodness and spiritual authority. I want to be part of that company named by Elizabeth A. Johnson that stretches backward and forward in time and encircles the globe in space. Thank you for walking this journey with me. May you also heal your intergenerational trauma and claim your spiritual authority. Kathe Schaaf offers this reminder:

> Maybe this is the real frontier for Western
> women at the intersection of spirituality and
> leadership—to first individually and then
> collectively overcome the fear that is written in
> our bones so that we can reclaim our natural

spiritual authority and bring our gifts of loving leadership to this struggling planetary family before it is too late. Maybe this is why—and how—the world could be saved by Western women. (227)

Our cosmos demands nothing less of us.

Now, Grünthrad and I again meet under our "Grandmother Oak." Again, it is a beautiful day. But today, after three years, I know this brave, strong woman at a much deeper level than I could have when she came into my presence asking, "Kannst du mi vehieren?"

During these three years, we have indeed "heard" each other and discovered a powerful bond of family between us. We have both grown and changed.

I begin, "Grünthrad, have you thought about the next steps of our journey together?"

After a brief pause, she replies, "I came to you feeling distraught and unable to rest. As you know, I kept roaming the land, especially the place where my family was killed. I was searching for some consolation, but nothing came. Then I felt your longing, that you needed me as much as I needed you. I could sense your desire to find out about our family so that you, too, could heal. I am so glad we found each other under this beautiful oak tree."

"I agree. I am so happy we connected. I didn't even know I needed you or my other ancestors, but you have brought me the richness and strength that I have needed," I said. "Now that I feel part of my larger family, I can ask for your help, consolation, wisdom, and resilience."

After a pause, I ask, "So, what is next? Do you need to leave?"

Grünthrad replies, "I can rest now, but that doesn't mean that we cannot talk with each other. I would hope that can continue. I don't want to lose you again."

"I don't either," I answer. "I will depend on you to inspire me with your wisdom and challenge me to be brave in speaking my spiritual authority. This is so urgent at this moment in our country. Goodbye for now."

"Goodbye," Grünthrad tells me, and she goes.

I am glad that she can rest now.

And I know that I will speak to her again soon.

ACKNOWLEDGMENTS

Thank you to all the people who will read this book, take it to heart, and choose to work with others to make the world a better place.

Special thanks go to these wonderful people who made this book possible:

- my religious community, the Franciscan Sisters of Perpetual Adoration (FSPA), who supported me throughout, and recognized this book as part of our mission to the world;
- FSPA affiliates and partners in mission, who inspire me every day with their goodness;
- my family members, who are always there for me and love nothing more than engaging in challenging, informative, and invigorating conversations;
- my long-term readers, hand-holders, and encouragers, who kept me going for three years of researching, writing, and growing:
    - Jane Comeau—FSPA director of communications and good friend, who early on recognized the importance of this topic, used her skills to give it legs, and shared coffee and conversation about all important things under the sun;
    - my brother and sister-in-law, Leon Lueck and Jean Oberbroeckling, who used their expertise in

communication, debate, and language skills and their own personal questioning to refine my ideas and expand my horizons;

- my good friends Mary Ellen and Bob Dunford, who provided a home space where I could be vulnerable and claim my true self. I am especially grateful (although sometimes grudgingly) to Mary Ellen, for her tough love in shaping Grünthrad's presence in this book and in my life;

- my other readers and encouragers along the way (you know who you are) who gave great feedback and cheered me on;

- Margie Law, my good friend from Seattle, who just happened to know "a woman who owns a publishing company." What are the chances of that? And it has made all the difference.

- Girl Friday Productions in Seattle, the woman-led organization that helped me publish my book and has been a godsend. Thanks especially to Kim Kent for holding my hand and managing all things publishing; to Shari MacDonald Strong, my developmental editor, who was so in sync with me and this book that it all felt seamless; to Katie Meyers, my marketing manager, who worked so hard helping me to get this book out into the world; to Alyssa Brillinger for patiently putting all the pieces together; and to all the other people behind the scenes who performed miracles.

- Carole Sargent, who helped me begin my publishing journey;

- Finally, the three coffee shops in La Crosse and Onalaska, Wisconsin, where I spent much of these last three years—Jules Coffee House, Cabin Coffee, and Barnes and Noble Café.

BIBLIOGRAPHY

Atkinson, James. "Reformation." In *Introduction to the History of Christianity*. 2nd ed. Edited by Tim Dowley. Minneapolis: Fortress Press, 2013.

Blackie, Sharon. *If Women Rose Rooted: The Journey to Authenticity and Belonging*. Tewkesbury, England: September Publishing, 2016.

Brown, Brené. *I Thought It Was Just Me (But It Isn't): Making the Journey from "What Will People Think?" to "I Am Enough."* New York: Avery (an imprint of Penguin Random House), 2007.

Brown, Peter. *The Rise of Western Christendom: Triumph and Diversity, AD 200–1000*. 2nd ed. Malden, MA: Blackwell Publishing, 2003.

Brueggemann, Walter. *Reality, Grief, Hope: Three Urgent Prophetic Tasks*. Grand Rapids, MN: William B. Eerdmans Publishing, 2014.

Canton, James. *The Oak Papers*. New York: HarperCollins Publishers, 2020.

Cepress, Celestine, ed. *Sister Thea Bowman, Shooting Star: Selected Writings and Speeches*. Franciscan Sisters of Perpetual Adoration, 1993.

Clouse, Robert G. "Flowering: The Western Church." In *Introduction to the History of Christianity*. 2nd ed. Edited by Tim Dowley. Minneapolis: Fortress Press, 2013.

Cusack, Carole. "Pagan Saxon Resistance to Charlemagne's Mission: 'Indigenous' Religion and 'World' Religion in the Early Middle Ages," in *The Pomegranate: The International Journal of Pagan Studies*, 2011.

Depew, Jennifer. "'The Glorious American Banner Floating High Above the Ramparts': The Rise and Fall of Know-Nothingism in Wisconsin." *Oshkosh Scholar*. 2018.

Detzler, Wayne A. "Europe in Revolt." In *Introduction to the History of Christianity*. 2nd ed. Edited by Tim Dowley. Minneapolis: Fortress Press, 2013.

Dulle, Colleen. "The German Synodal Way, Explained." *America Magazine*. June 24, 2021.

Ellsberg, Robert. "Blessed Among Us." *Give Us This Day: Daily Prayers for Today's Catholic*. Collegeville, MN: Liturgical Press, April 10, 2021; October 4, 2023; November 29, 2024.

Enns, Elaine, and Ched Myers. *Healing Haunted Histories: A Settler Discipleship of Decolonization*. Eugene, Oregon: Cascade Books, 2021.

Estés, Clarissa Pinkola. *Women Who Run with the Wolves*. New York: Ballantine Books, 1992.

Fox, Matthew. *Julian of Norwich: Wisdom in a Time of Pandemic—and Beyond*. Bloomington, IN: iUniverse, 2020.

_____. *Original Blessing: A Primer in Creation Spirituality*. Rochester, Vermont: Bear and Company, 1983.

Gies, Frances and Joseph. *Women in the Middle Ages: The Real Lives of Women in a Vibrant Age of Transition*. New York: HarperCollins Publishers, 1998, 2018.

Goldsmith, Martin. *Alex's Wake: A Voyage of Betrayal and a Journey of Remembrance*. Boston: Da Capo Press, 2014.

Herman, Judith. *Trauma and Recovery: The Aftermath of Violence—from Domestic Abuse to Political Terror*. New York: Basic Books, 1992.

Herring, Laraine. "Ancestors as Source." In *Writing Begins with the Breath: Embodying Your Authentic Voice*. Boston: Shambhala Publications, 2007.

Horan, Daniel. "How History Will Judge the Church Harshly

for Its Treatment of LGBTQ Persons." *National Catholic Reporter*. February 9, 2022.

Horsley, Kate. *Confessions of a Pagan Nun*. Boston: Shambhala Publications, 2001.

Houck, James A., Jr. *When Ancestors Weep: Healing the Soul from Intergenerational Trauma*. Bloomington, IN: Abbott Press, 2018.

Hübl, Thomas. *Healing Collective Trauma: A Process for Integrating Our Intergenerational and Cultural Wounds*. Boulder, CO: Sounds True, 2020.

Hughes, Marianne, in Linda Lowen's article "The Dalai Lama— 'The World Will Be Saved by the Western Woman,'" https://www.thoughtco.com/dalai-lama-world-saved-western-women-3971297, updated February 28, 2019.

Jackson, Regina, and Saira Rao. *White Women: Everything You Already Know About Your Own Racism and How to Do Better*. New York: Penguin Books, 2022.

Janik, Erika. "A Short History of Wisconsin." Wisconsin Historical Society Press, 2012.

Johnson, Elizabeth A. *Friends of God and Prophets: A Feminist Theological Reading of the Communion of Saints*. New York: Continuum, 1998.

_____. *She Who Is: The Mystery of God in Feminist Theological Discourse*. New York: The Crossroad Publishing Company, 1992.

King, Martin Luther, Jr. *Why We Can't Wait*. New York: Harper and Row, 1964.

Knipper, Kathy. "The Gift of Ancestral Rootedness." *You Will Have Light for Your First Steps: A Reflective Journal on Discernment*. Leadership Conference of Women Religious, 2020.

Kobes Du Mez, Kristin. *Jesus and John Wayne: How White Evangelicals Corrupted a Faith and Fractured a Nation*. New York: W. W. Norton, 2020.

Koch, Carl. *A Popular History of the Catholic Church.* Winona, MN: Saint Mary's Press, 1997.

Kozak, Pat. In *Give Us This Day.* September 29, 2024.

Levack, Brian P., ed. *The Oxford Handbook of Witchcraft in Early Modern Europe and Colonial America.* Oxford, England: Oxford University Press, 2013.

Linder, Robert D. "The Catholic Reformation." In *Introduction to the History of Christianity.* 2nd ed. Edited by Tim Dowley. Minneapolis: Fortress Press, 2013.

Lorde, Audre. *Sister Outsider.* Crossing Press, 1984.

Lueck, Karen. *Cheering for the Good: Leading When It Matters.* Denver: Outskirts Press, 2021.

Markuly, Mark. "The Experience of Fear in Our Churches." In *A Matter of Spirit* (the newsletter for the Intercommunity Peace and Justice Center, Seattle, WA). No. 112, Fall 2016.

McBrien, Richard P. *Catholicism: New Edition.* New York: HarperCollins Publishers, 1994.

McConahay, Mary Jo. *Playing God: American Catholic Bishops and the Far Right.* Brooklyn, NY: Melville House, 2022.

McElroy, Cardinal Robert. "Disclosing God's Love." In www.ncronline.org, November 14, 2023.

McLaren, Brian D. *Do I Stay Christian?: A Guide for the Doubters, the Disappointed, and the Disillusioned.* New York: St. Martin's Essentials (an imprint of St. Martin's Publishing Group), 2022.

McNair, Philip. "Seeds of Renewal." In *Introduction to the History of Christianity.* 2nd ed. Edited by Tim Dowley. Minneapolis: Fortress Press, 2013.

McNamara, Jo Ann Kay. *Sisters in Arms: Catholic Nuns Through Two Millennia.* Cambridge, MA: Harvard University Press, 1996.

Menaken, Resmaa. *My Grandmother's Hands: Racialized Trauma and the Pathway to Mending Our Hearts and Bodies.* Las Vegas: Central Recovery Press, 2017.

Merelli, Annalisa, "A History of American Anti-Immigrant Bias, Starting with Benjamin Franklin's Hatred of the Germans" in *Quartz*, July 20, 2022.

Mescher, Bob, and Laverne Bockenstedt, eds. *Unity in Community: St. Boniface Parish Sesquicentennial 1845–1995 and New Vienna Centenniul 1895–1995*. New Vienna, IA, 1995.

Nakashima Brock, Rita, and Rebecca Ann Parker. *Saving Paradise: How Christianity Traded Love of This World for Crucifixion and Empire*. Boston: Beacon Press, 2008.

New Revised Standard Version Bible. New York: Oxford University Press, 1989.

Impelli, Matthew. "Priest Calls for Pope Francis to Be Killed, Likens Him to the Devil." Newsweek, October 20, 2023, https:// newsweek.com/priest-calls-pope-francis-killed -likens-him-devil-1836438.

Rohr, Richard. *Eager to Love: The Alternative Way of Francis of Assisi*. Cincinnati, OH: Franciscan Media, 2014.

Rosenberg, Harry. "The West in Crisis." In *Introduction to the History of Christianity*. 2nd ed. Edited by Tim Dowley. Minneapolis: Fortress Press, 2013.

Russell, James C. *The Germanization of Early Medieval Christianity: A Sociohistorical Approach to Religious Transformation*. New York: Oxford University Press, 1994.

Sanders, Annmarie, ed. *However Long the Night: Making Meaning in a Time of Crisis*. Washington, D.C.: Leadership Conference of Women Religious, 2018.

Sass, Robert. *Saxon Paganism for Today*. Lulu.com, 2015.

Schaaf, Kathe. "Written in My Bones." In *Women, Spirituality, and Transformative Leadership: Where Grace Meets Power*, Schaaf, Lindahl, Hurty, and Cheen, eds. Woodstock, VT: Skylight Paths Publishing, 2012.

Schaller, Tom, and Paul Waldman. *White Rural Rage: The Threat to American Democracy*. New York: Random House, 2024.

Scheer, Teva J. *Our Daily Bread: Village Life in Early Modern Germany.* North Saanich, BC, Canada: Adventis Press, 2010.

Seidel, Andrew L., and Amanda Tyler, eds. *Christian Nationalism and the January 6, 2021 Insurrection.* Collaboration Report from the Baptist Joint Committee for Religious Liberty (BJC) and Freedom from Religion Foundation (FFRF), 2002.

Sharratt, Mary. *Illuminations: A Novel of Hildegard von Bingen.* New York: Mariner Books (Houghton Mifflin Harcourt), 2012.

Sieghart, Mary Ann. *The Authority Gap: Why Women Are Still Taken Less Seriously Than Men, and What We Can Do About It.* New York: W. W. Norton, 2021.

Skenandore, Amanda. *Between Earth and Sky.* New York: Kensington Books, 2018.

Smith, Charlene, and John Feister. *Thea's Song: The Life of Thea Bowman.* Maryknoll, NY: Orbis Books, 2009.

Sölle, Dorothee. *The Silent Cry: Mysticism and Resistance.* Minneapolis: Fortress Press, 2001.

Solnit, Rebecca. Essay written in 2008 in *Men Explain Things to Me.* Chicago: Haymarket Books, 2014.

Stevens-Arroyo, Anthony M. "Civilization and Religion: The Dance of Shape-Shifters." In *Comparative Civilizations Review*, vol. 64, Spring 2011.

Stewart, Katherine. *The Power Worshippers: Inside the Dangerous Rise of Religious Nationalism.* New York: Bloomsbury Publishing, 2019.

Stuart, Gary. *Healing Human History: Constellation Wisdom for the 21st Century.* Self-published, 2020.

Swan, Laura, *The Wisdom of the Beguines: The Forgotten Story of a Medieval Women's Movement.* Golden Bridge, NY: Blue Bridge Books, 2014.

Szabados, Stephen. *German Immigration to America: When, Why, How, and Where.* Self-published, 2020.

Tholking, John, and Josef Borgerding. "Vechta (Oldenburg)—Cincinnati Genealogy." In *The Tracer* (Hamilton County Genealogical Society), June 2012.

Warner, Steven C. "Wake the World with Dawning Joy." Music and lyrics commissioned by NRVC and VISION Vocation Guide in honor of the World Day of Consecrated Life. Franklin Park, IL: World Library Publications, 2014.

Watterson, Meggan. *Mary Magdalene Revealed: The First Apostle, Her Feminist Gospel and the Christianity We Haven't Tried Yet*. Carlsbad, CA: Hay House, 2019.

Whitehead, Andrew L., and Samuel L. Perry. *Taking America Back for God: Christian Nationalism in the United States*. New York: Oxford University Press, 2020, 2022.

Winter, Miriam Therese. *Paradoxology: Spirituality in a Quantum Universe*. Maryknoll, NY: Orbis Books, 2009.

Worley, Savannah. "Dear White Women: Here's Why It's Hard to Be Friends with You." In *An Injustice! Magazine*, April 19, 2021.

ABOUT THE AUTHOR

© Diane Knothe at Apropos Photography

KAREN LUECK is a Franciscan Sister of Perpetual Adoration (FSPA) based in La Crosse, Wisconsin. She grew up on a farm in eastern Iowa and has a master's degree in pastoral counseling from Loyola University in Chicago and a doctorate in ministry with an emphasis in women's theology and psychology from Chicago Theological Seminary. In her ministry, she has served as an elementary school teacher and principal, mental health counselor, spiritual director, novice director, and leader of her religious community. In all her ministries, Karen Lueck focused on seeing the goodness in the people with whom she served. Her first book, *Cheering for the Good: Leading When It Matters*, carried out this deeply held commitment. Her second book, *The Green Thread*, continues urging readers to claim their inner goodness and spiritual authority.

www.ingramcontent.com/pod-product-compliance
Lightning Source LLC
Chambersburg PA
CBHW021709120626
46545CB00004B/1478